A COLLECTOR'S GUIDE TO

D O L L S

KERRY TAYLOR

A COLLECTOR'S GUIDE TO

D O L L S

WELLFLEET
PRESS

MAI   273   1919

To Jon, Thomas and B.B.

<u>A COLLECTOR'S GUIDE TO DOLLS</u>
First published in 1990 by Wellfleet Books
an imprint of Book Sales, Inc.
110 Enterprise Avenue
Secaucus, New Jersey 07094

Copyright © 1990 Studio Editions Ltd.

This book was designed and edited by Anness Law Limited
42 Carnaby Street, London W1V 1PD

The author and publishers would like to thank everyone in the Collectors' Department at Sotheby's London for their help.

Editor: Patricia Bayer
Designer: David Rowley
Picture Researcher: Claudia Brigg

ISBN 1-55521-545-9

Printed and bound in Czechoslovakia

<u>Publisher's note</u>
Prices for dolls sold at specific auctions are given in £ sterling followed by US$ prices in parantheses at the exchange rate pertaining on the day of sale. All other prices are calculated at an exchange rate of £0.606 to US$1.

CONTENTS

INTRODUCTION

Doll collecting, once a sedate pastime practised by a few refined ladies, is today one of the largest and fastest-growing collecting fields in the world. In commercial terms, the buying and selling of dolls constitutes an extremely valuable business; in fact, a recent American survey showed doll collecting second only to philately—quite a feat, since stamp collecting has been around for so much longer. Although dolls have been collected since the nineteenth century, it was only in the 1920s that major collections were formed and proper research into the field was instituted. Even so, there is still a great deal to learn about the origins, techniques of manufacture and various sources of the many different kinds of dolls. With every passing year, more information comes to light as new trade journals are discovered and as specialist collectors generously share their knowledge which has been gleaned from hours of painstaking research.

The aim of this book is to present the reader with the most up-to-date data on all aspects of doll collecting, including all-important market information. As the prices of some dolls spiral upward, it is important, too, for collectors to be aware of the many pitfalls of buying, selling, and trading in general, since mistakes can prove costly. At the time of going to press, the world record price for a doll was £90,200 ($141,600),

achieved at Sotheby's in London in February 1989 for a rare Kämmer & Reinhardt character doll, made in Germany c.1910 and impressed with the mould number 105. Not a particularly attractive doll, it had a very small production run (probably due to its unprepossessing face) and was thus very rare indeed—hence the enormous price. As more and more collectors join the field to compete for the ever-lessening supply of dolls, it is only a question of time before individual dolls soar past the six-figure barrier. Looked at from a purely financial or investment point of view this is extremely good news for those who already own fine doll collections, but novices need not be deterred: for those trying to build up collections there are still undervalued, underappreciated areas, many of which will be pointed out in the following pages. In the highly competitive doll market it is still possible to find a bargain, but only if you know what you are doing. Collectors with a good all-round knowledge of their subject are more likely to pick up the bargains than someone who buys on impulse without investing much time or thought in the matter. Although this book will show the reader some of the more sought-after rarities, it will not concentrate exclusively on these. Not all collectors can afford the thousands needed to buy a French Jumeau bisque doll, supposing even that it was to their taste, so the cheaper and

Oil painting of three sisters, early seventeenth century, circle of Robert Peake, fl 1598–1626.

more accessible end of the doll market will be covered as well.

If you ask doll collectors why they collect or what started them off on their collections, their answers will be many, diverse, and often highly personal. Over the many years spent working in the auction rooms, I have come into contact with literally thousands of collectors and tens of thousands of their dolls. For some, each doll is a personal friend, given its own name and life history and regarded as a member of the family. Some collectors who suffered the deprivations of a childhood during the Depression wish to compensate for this dreadful time by indulging themselves with the dolls they yearned for as a child, but which were then out of reach. Other collectors relate how they came across a single doll in an antiques sale or shop, and once that one was possessed the collecting bug became firmly embedded and hundreds more followed. Other collectors had inherited a single family doll and, in the course of finding out more about its history and method of manufacture, also became smitten by the doll-collecting bug. I myself became interested in dolls because for me they encapsulate the style of a particular period better than any other medium. Upon examining a Victorian dress, for example, you will learn something about the discomfort of clothing during that period, as well as the colours, textures,

and types of fabric popular at that specific time; a painting, on the other hand, will give an idea of the visual ambience of the time. But a doll combines all these factors—and often more. Dolls are a three-dimensional rendering in miniature of the human form and as such reflect the tastes and fashions prevalent at the time they were made: fatness, thinness, blonde or dark hair, fair or dark skin.

An interesting exercise is to look at a Georgian wooden doll—with its aristocratically severe face, hard black enamelled eyes, long neck, straight, slender torso, and elongated limbs—and then to compare it to a Bru Jeune bisque doll, with its peaches-and-cream glazed complexion, deep paperweight eyes, curling blonde wig, and generously chubby proportions. By contrasting the two we can see clearly how the idea of what constitutes beauty changes from age to age. Human images made by man manifest a mysterious truthfulness and honesty, showing as they do the maker's real idea of himself and his fellow humans.

Indeed, just as out of the mouths of babes great wisdom often can be spouted, so from the dolls of children's play a great deal can be learned of the fashions and social history of their time.

For as long as there have been children doubtless dolls and playthings also have existed. In a sense dolls can be seen to chart many of the technological advances of the past centuries. Primitive dolls excavated on archaeological digs are made of the cheapest indigenous substances, usually clay, bone, or some type of local stone. As man's skill in metal-working increased so small bronze and iron figures appeared. Beautifully modelled and detailed clay figures of the fourteenth and fifteenth centuries have survived, although wood seems to have been the most popular of all materials used for early dolls. There are numerous portraits of children dating from the sixteenth century in which the young child is depicted holding a turned wooden doll. They usually take the form of lady dolls dressed in sumptuous materials, often echoing the costume of the child. Only portraits of noblemen's children with their beloved dolls are extant today for us to inspect, but no doubt the children of peasants cherished just as dearly their own simple skittle dolls wrapped in pieces of rag.

The individual stamp of affection that each child leaves on his or her toy is one of the main qualities that makes dolls so appealing. Dolls that still retain the clothes carefully hand-sewn by the little girl who owned them have enormous charm, be they 1850s printed-cotton dresses with matching underclothes and bonnet, or the knitted outfit a little child has attempted for her Käthe Kruse rag doll in the 1920s. Some dolls brought into the salerooms have come complete with handwritten life histories detailing who has owned them and when. Sometimes the tales are heartbreaking, with little Annie dying of consumption at the age of six; sometimes the tales are endearing, relating how a doll helped and supported its tiny owner through hard times. Indeed, it is a shame that more dolls are not sold with their full provenances. For many lonely elderly people, it is important that their beloved childhood friend be passed on to a new

A Daniel et Cie Bébé doll (**above**), *French, c. 1889, with composition and jointed wood body, closed smiling mouth and fixed brown glass paperweight eyes, cream satin dress, maroon velvet jacket, leather shoes and fine cream silk parasol.*
35in (89cm)
£12000 ($18840), Sotheby's London, 1989

Three waxed composition pumpkin head dolls and a bonnet head doll (**left**), *German, c. 1860, all with cloth bodies and wooden lower limbs.*
The largest 9½in (24cm), the smallest 8¼in (21cm)
£194 ($310) sold as a lot, Sotheby's London 1989

A Simon and Halbig bisque doll (above), German, c. 1892, with composition and jointed wood body, brown glass eyes, dark real hair, black dress decorated with white crochet and hat.
33in (84cm)
£418 ($655), Sotheby's London 1989

A Jumeau Triste bisque doll (left), French, c. 1875, with composition and jointed wood body, blue glass paperweight eyes, real blonde hair wig on cork pate, open closed mouth, cream cut silk and silk-lined clothing.
27½in (70cm)
£6000 ($9420), Sotheby's London 1989

owner who, if not lavishing it with the love and affection it has known, at least respects the special place it has occupied in its first owner's life. But it must be noted—looking at things with a cold, commercial eye —that untouched, unloved dolls, left in their original clothes and kept in their original boxes, command far higher prices than their much-handled contemporaries. So when bestowing love and affection on your dolls, remember to do so with care!

This book has been separated into easily accessible sections, starting with individual chapters arranged according to the various materials out of which dolls are made. Each chapter will clearly show the countries of manufacture, body construction, and different types of head, eyes, limbs, and dress for the various materials employed. In this way you should be able to ascertain if the doll you own has the correct head for its body. Unfortunately, fakes have come onto the market over the past few years and many buyers have bought what they thought was a rare doll at a cheap price, only to find out that they have been duped. There is a small but important section in the Buyer's Guide on how to spot the fake doll. Also at the end of the book are sections on recording, cataloguing, photographing, storing and displaying your collection, with a helpful glossary of technical terms.

WOODEN DOLLS

THE WORLD OF WOODEN DOLLS

OFFERS WONDERFUL SCOPE FOR

BOTH THE NEW AND THE

ESTABLISHED COLLECTOR.

THEY RANGE IN PRICE FROM THE

VERY INEXPENSIVE TO THE MOST

VALUABLE OF ALL COLLECTABLE

DOLLS.

Wooden dolls are perhaps one of the most exciting areas of doll collecting, mainly because little real information about early examples exists and so there remains much scope for research. Often inaccurately referred to as Queen Anne dolls, wooden dolls were largely produced in Georgian England throughout the eighteenth century and well into the nineteenth (Anne reigned only from 1702 to 1714, hence the misuse of that historical description for these dolls).

As more and more dolls come to light (which recent high prices in the salerooms have encouraged), definite types of wooden dolls are emerging, some with original costumes, a factor enabling experts to date the doll styles more accurately. Most early wooden dolls seem to have been made in England, although Italy and southern Germany also produced wooden dolls. The Continental examples tend to date from the late eighteenth century and are much more finely carved and detailed than their English counterparts. The style of carving is more in keeping with the ecclesiastical carvings produced in those countries. The faces and hands in particular are beautifully detailed, with less attention paid to the bodies. Indeed some of these figures lack legs altogether, sporting only simple skirt-

shaped cages of wood for support. Some also have extremely well-carved hairstyles, whereas the English dolls without exception have nailed-on wigs. However, Italian and south German dolls are less desirable to collectors than the more naïve English wooden examples, which are generally regarded as the very best of their type.

Little is known about the skilled craftsmen who made these wooden dolls, which were luxury playthings aimed at the children of the aristocracy. One possibility is that picture-frame makers, who were called in to the great houses to produce elaborate

*The Old Pretender, a fine carved wooden doll (**above left**), English, c. 1695, with the head applied with decorative patches, and wearing elaborate fontange headdress.*
13in (33cm)
Bethnal Green Museum, London

*A pair of carved and painted wooden creche figures, (**right**), German, late eighteenth century, with emphasized hands, elaborate silk and braided costumes.*
14¹/₂in (37cm)
Münchner Stadtmuseum

A pair of rare painted wood religious figures (left), south German, late eighteenth century, with open-work caged skirt supports.
45in (114cm) and 44in (112cm)
£1430 ($2260), Sotheby's London 1989

Lord and Lady Clapham, a fine pair of wooden dolls (right), English, c. 1690, with original outfits and accessories. Victoria & Albert Museum, London

frames in which to mount the family portraits, also could have provided dolls for the children. They possessed the necessary painting and woodcarving skills and were well used to handling gesso. However, many great houses possessed their own workshops for producing furniture and for repairing and restoring various items in the house, so a turned wooden doll would be 'child's play' for an experienced carpenter, whose time would have been spent on more important tasks. I think the possibility that skilled woodcarvers doubled as doll-makers rather unlikely, as so many of these dolls have a common feel to them, with similar constructional and facial characteristics that probably resulted from their being produced in the same commercial workshops. It may well be that there were major workshops producing the dolls, which were subsequently sold throughout England and elsewhere in Europe by travelling journeymen. Unfortunately, no documentary evidence has yet come to light to

prove this last possibility, but many experts are convinced it is the most likely explanation.

Perhaps the most famous of all wooden dolls are a pair of male and female figures sold by Sotheby's on 19 April 1974 which are today in the collection of the Victoria and Albert Museum, London. 'Lord and Lady Clapham', as they were known to their original owners and are still called today, were purchased for the sum of £16,000 ($26,400), at the time a fortune. They are not only outstanding examples of late seventeenth-century dolls, but they are also excellent costume figures. Lady Clapham wears a cap with lappets (trailing side ribbons) and a fontange (a kind of headdress) of wired frill, giving her extra height. A silver stomacher adorns her front, and her ivory silk gown is in the rare form of a mantua. Mantuas were very popular in the early part of the eighteenth century, but few have survived unaltered due to many being adapted to form sack-backed gowns later in the century. The skirt train is doubled over and held in place by loops and silk-covered buttons. Although rarely found in adult dress, it is unique as an item of doll costume. Lord Clapham wears a scarlet wool knee-length coat with flared skirt, a tricorn hat, and a silver brocade waistcoat. They are also accompanied by a chest containing a large quantity of accessories, underwear, and undress robes (informal wear).

The heads of both dolls are large in proportion to their bodies, a feature of dolls from the late seventeenth to early eighteenth century. They have carved wooden oval faces covered with a thin layer of gesso (liquid plaster) that has been delicately painted. Their general expressions are soft and amiable, unlike the harder features of later dolls. The head and torso are carved in one piece, with jointed wooden limbs applied. Both dolls have applied hair wigs, but neither has any details for ears.

A lady doll with facial features similar to those of the Claphams—and probably produced by the same hands—is housed in the Bethnal Green Museum in London. Known as the 'Old Pretender', because she was supposedly given by the family of James Stuart to the family of a supporter, the doll has a disproportionately large head with delicately carved features, painted upward-glancing eyes, slightly feathered eyebrows, and four enormous black beauty patches. The fontange headdress on this doll is even more spectacular than that on Lady Clapham, and her wooden fork-like hands are covered in kid leather to impart a more realistic fleshy feel. Yet another late seventeenth-century wooden doll forms part of the costume collection of Amsterdam's Rijksmuseum. Unfortunately, this particular doll was re-dressed in a costume of striped silk in the 1740s.

Most eighteenth-century dolls take the form of lady dolls, and to a lesser degree male dolls. Although a small wooden baby doll was supposed to have formed part of the original Clapham collection, it is a crudely carved example and probably an addition made by a child from a successive generation. Indeed, child dolls are very rare, and many deemed as such are actually

A fine George II wooden doll, c. 1735, with dotted lashes and brows over a single line, nailed auburn wig, the torso with legs jointed at the knee and ending in block feet, cloth upper arms and wooden forearms with long fork fingers in gold silk sack-backed gown and ribbed silk shoes.

26in (66cm), restored
£5500 ($8690), Sotheby's London 1989

A rare George II wooden doll, English c. 1710–1735, with painted gessoed face, inserted black glass eyes, delicately painted lashes and feathered brows, linen wig with real hair, lined bonnet, cap and ribbed petticoat. 29in (74cm) £38000 ($59660), Sotheby's London 1989

A George II wooden doll, English c. 1740, with lashes and brows of short brushstrokes, auburn wig, the torso with accentuated waist, squared hips and simple straight tapering legs ending in block feet, cloth upper arms and wooden forearms, in original olive silk and satin gown. 11¾in (30cm) £3520 ($5560), Sotheby's London 1989

smaller versions of lady dolls that were never intended to represent children.

The second clearly recognizable group of wooden dolls appeared around 1700–40. These dolls have more rounded faces of carved wood with gessoed, varnished complexions. Instead of painted eyes, they feature enamelled glass eyes inserted into elliptical slits cut into the head. The eyes are wide and narrow, with large black pupils, no irises, and very little white showing on either side. The mouth, a wide red slit with small, heart-shaped lip details at the centre, is positioned very closely below the nose. The doll has a pronounced forehead, very little chin, and a long, wide neck. These dolls are often clad in gowns of single-coloured taffeta, for example of Chinese yellow, or at times their dress comprises patchwork strips of left-over fancy fabric, perhaps in shades of gold and green. They wear simple unadorned stomachers and sometimes wide pannier-sided skirts. The gowns are generally less fussy and frilly than those worn by mid-eighteenth-century dolls. As on the earlier examples, the dolls have wooden fork-like hands, although the arms are often attached to the body by strips of leather rather than joints.

By the mid-eighteenth century, dolls' heads became more proportionate to their bodies, although the necks and sloping shoulders seem longer than ever. The eyebrows of these dolls are often in a herringbone pattern and elongated to match the eyes. Still quite wide in relation to the rest of the face, the enamelled glass eyes have become slightly rounder. Carved wooden ears often appear on dolls of this date, and hair is again applied by being nailed to the head. Body construction is similar to that of dolls a decade or so earlier, but the feet are now slightly longer. Instead of having only stubs to suggest feet, good-quality dolls feature individually carved toes, as well as detailed carved fingernails on the hands. The gowns are normally open robes, with a petticoat showing at the front. Those of the 1750s are more elaborate, often trimmed with lace, gauze, large flounced engageants (elbow frills), fly braid, pinked bands of ribbons, and decorative flounces of fabric called furbelows. There is a much greater use of brocades

with tenon-jointed limbs. Dolls' gowns from this period are often of brocaded silk, generally sack-backed (where pleats of fabric fall from the shoulders to the back of the dress), but the design in the fabric is quite subdued, with small floral repeats.

Wooden dolls produced from around 1780 to the end of the eighteenth century have more of a skittle-shaped head and torso. Less attention was paid to making the dolls look realistic. The wide enamelled eyes are now more closely set, with dot-to-dot outlining on the eyebrows and lashes taking precedence over feathered strokes. The eyebrows almost meet above the nose and form long arcs over the eyes. The lips are tighter, assuming more of a rosebud shape. The hairstyles are extremely elaborate in the late 1770s and 1780s. They are large affairs, often powdered or grey (looking young at this point was very unfashionable) and piled up in large bangs on top of the head and at both sides. Hair adornments were very popular, as were accessories such as feathered headdresses, ribbons, and large silk bonnets.

In the 1790s and early 1800s dolls' heads continued to be made in the aforementioned skittle shape, and the bodies became even more elongated and slim. A tiny mouth, close-set eyes and eyebrows are commonplace, as are heavily rouged circles on the cheeks. Eyes now tend to be blue as well as black, with the blue-enamelled eyes having tiny black specks for pupils. The feet were getting longer by the turn of the century, and many dolls sported kid leather lower arms instead of the usual wooden hands and lower arms. The 'milkmaid' look, as promoted by Marie Antoinette before her sad demise, was very fashionable and dolls are often found dressed in romantic, softly draped muslins, with wide fichus covering the breasts. By 1800 the bustline had ascended and the waistline vanished. Dolls of this date have quite a tubular appearance, often with outsized feet, and are dressed in country chintzes and muslins. By 1800 the hairstyles on the dolls became very simple, often comprising no more than strands of hair attached as a fringe to the top of the head. Sometimes white goat-kid fleece is applied to the head, which produces a very curly, short hairstyle that looks very attractive.

By the early nineteenth century, English wooden dolls lost their popularity. It is still possible to find good examples as late as the 1820s, but these are rare. The general naïveté and lack of realism of these dolls caused them to fall from favour, especially as the more elegant, slender, long-limbed wooden peg dolls from the Austrian and Bavarian Tyrol were exported in increasingly large numbers. These dolls are referred to by collectors as Grödnertals, although some were obviously produced outside this area in Austria, probably in Sonneberg, Thüringia, and other well-known German toy- and doll-making regions. Grödnertals date from between 1800 and 1830. One of the best-loved and best-known collections of Grödnertal dolls

A George III wooden doll **(above),** *English, c. 1780, with dotted eyelashes and eyebrows, fair wool wig, the torso slightly tapered at waist, crudely carved hips and legs jointed at hip and knee, cloth upper and wooden lower arms in figured silk polonaise gown.*
15in (38cm) £4400 ($6950), Sotheby's London 1989

A George II wooden doll **(left),** *English, c. 1759–1769, with feather painted eyebrows, the torso with tapered waist, rounded hips, and legs jointed at the hip and knee, disc jointed at shoulder and elbow. 18in (46cm), restored, £9350 ($14775), Sotheby's London 1989*

(woven, coloured, patterned silks) at this date, reflecting the adult fashions of the time. The émigré Huguenot weavers had set up looms in the Spitalfields area of London, and consequently many of the dolls are found dressed in their rich fabrics.

In the 1760s and 1770s dolls' heads were smaller than before. The eyes are even more elongated, with feathering to the eyebrows a commonplace. The mouth is less wide but thin, while the forehead is very pronounced. Ears are often carved in one piece, with the head and wig tied back tightly to frame the face. Overall the face is more severe and the neck and shoulders long and sloping, giving the doll an elegant, aristocratic demeanour. Hands and feet are well carved, some with thorn-like ankles. The better quality dolls have circular ball joints at the elbows and knees

*Two George III wooden
dolls, English,
c. 1790–1810, with
painted faces, rouged
cheeks, inserted eyes, dotted
eyelashes and eyebrows,
nailed-on wigs and muslin
dresses with satin borders.
17in (43cm) and
13in (33cm)
£1500 ($2370) and
£950 ($1500),
Sotheby's London 1989*

is that amassed by Queen Victoria as a child, part of which is housed in the Museum of London. The young princess and her governess, Baroness Lehzen, often dressed the dolls to represent different imaginary characters and theatrical stars.

A wind of change was blowing through Europe in the early nineteenth century. After the excesses of the French Revolution there was a desire for order, symmetry, and refined elegance. This was best reflected in Neoclassicism, the revival of ancient Greek art that was embraced by architects, dress-makers, painters, and indeed even by toy- and doll-makers. Women dressed in diaphanous white muslin gowns with high waistlines, and the look achieved was one of discreet, cool elegance, that is, assuming one had the tall, slim figure necessary for this style. The Grödnertal dolls, instead of being exclusive toys for the rich, were inexpensive to produce and thus were within the reach of most families—unlike the wooden dolls of the eighteenth century, which were commissioned and produced solely for the children of the upper class.

Grödnertal peg dolls were made of turned softwood, with heads and faces carved, gessoed, painted, and varnished. Their long wooden limbs were either pivoted or ball-jointed for ease of articulation. The lower arms and legs are normally painted, while the rest of the body is of plain wood.

Grödnertals vary widely in size, from between a mere ½in (1.3cm) to 40in (101cm) high. The larger examples are normally ball-jointed and often have a swivel joint at the waist. The early and large Grödnertals have superbly painted, expressive faces, with hair painted in tight, forward-flowing curls around the brow. The Grödnertals of the 1820s and '30s were produced for a larger mass market and have less well-painted but still most attractive faces. Large carved, painted, and often gilded haircombs sprout from the tops of their heads, to the sides of which earrings are pinned. Grödnertals dressed *c.*1800 wear high-waisted tubular dresses (as described earlier), and in the 1820s short puff sleeves begin to appear. These gradually become larger until by the 1830s they assume enor-

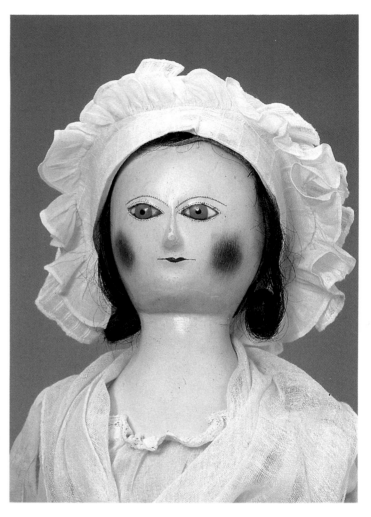

The head of a George III wooden doll, English, c. 1760, with feathered eyebrows, auburn wig, torso with formed breasts, tapered waist to angular hips, tenon-jointed knee and hip joints and well formed legs.
17in (43cm) £17,600 ($27810), Sotheby's London 1989

The head of a George III wooden doll, English, 1780–1800 with crudely carved body and slightly tapered waist, inserted blue enamelled eyes, dotted eyelashes and brows.
20in (51cm) £2310 ($3650), Sotheby's London 1989

mous, balloon shapes. By now the skirt is shorter and rounder, with the silhouette losing its tall, elegant lines of 1800 and taking on the wide, spinning-top shape of 1830.

Some Grödnertals are found dressed as pedlars, complete with trays of exquisitely made miniature wares, others as fortune-telling dolls, wearing paper skirts peppered with various amusing and dramatic omens in tiny script. Some dolls fill dainty little shoes, illustrating the popular nursery rhyme 'There was an old woman who lived in a shoe'.

After 1830 these charming little peg dolls fell completely from favour. As the hairstyles of the 1830s became larger and more elaborate, and as the accepted, fashionable shape for women became more curvaceous, other materials were deemed more suitable for modelling dolls than wood.

Although humble little peg dolls were probably played with by poorer children in the intervening years, they were not mass-produced in large numbers again until the turn of the twentieth century. In 1895

Florence Upton, born in New York of English parentage, produced her beautifully illustrated book on the adventures of two wooden peg dolls and a Golliwog, the latter of which she is credited with inventing. Peg dolls were once again back in fashion and tens of thousands were exported from Holland and Germany for sale all over Europe. These Dutch dolls, as they are called, are very crude skittle-shaped dolls with naïvely painted faces and simple jointed limbs. The faces have an altogether pinker or whiter complexion and are unvarnished (unlike the early Grödnertals, which have pleasantly yellowed faces due to the aged varnish with which they were finished). The Dutch dolls' heads are simply daubed with black paint, and there is no attempt at realistic portrayal. Entire wedding parties of these dolls have been discovered, dressed by their owner at the turn of the century. They are very inexpensive to buy, and it is highly probable that examples found in original costumes might prove a good investment for the future.

In 1872 Albert Schoenhut, a German émigré, in his

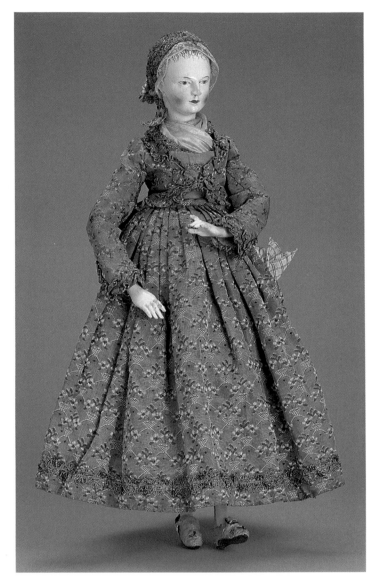

early 20s, opened his own toy factory in Philadelphia, Pennsylvania. He specialized in wooden toys, and tradition has it that his father and grandfather had been linked to the wooden toy industry in Germany. The American company quickly earned renown for producing circus animals and figures that were fully articulated and brightly painted, had inset glass eyes, and became known as the Humpty Dumpty Circus. They were amusing, attractive, and durable toys, widely distributed throughout the United States and Europe. Albert Schoenhut soon came to realize that there was

A collection of Grödnertal and wooden peg dolls (above),
from left to right, c. 1830, 1845–1850, 1820, 1830,
with shoes from 4¹/₄ to 9¹/₂in (11 to 42cm) long.
£880 ($1390), £1650 ($2610), £3200 ($1900) and
£825 ($1300), Sotheby's London 1989
A fine wooden doll (left), German, c. 1810, with
well-jointed wooden body, painted windswept hairstyle,
painted shoes and heavy brocaded gown.
£3250 ($5560), Sotheby's London 1989
A Schoenhut wooden doll (far left), American, c. 1925,
incised on the back SCHOENHUT DOLL, PAT.
JAN 17TH, USA & FOREIGN COUNTRIES, with
spring-jointed body, painted face with blue eyes, brown
bobbed moulded hair and a blue band.
14¹/₂in (37cm)
£550 ($975), Sotheby's London 1989

a gap in the doll market that he could exploit. The majority of dolls of this date were being produced in either bisque (matte-glazed porcelain) or brittle composition, both of which were easily breakable. One problem with bisque dolls was that, if dropped, their beautiful heads simply smashed. After hours of constant play the stringing became loose and the doll had to be repaired. Schoenhut believed that he could produce a robust, cleverly articulated doll for the twentieth-century child, a doll that would never need re-

stringing and that would stand up to the rigours of unsupervised play.

In 1909 he patented the first spring-jointed doll, later marketed as the Schoenhut 'All-Wood Perfection Art Doll'. Schoenhut already had the lathes and workrooms set up for producing the intricately jointed animals, so it was a simple step for him to start producing dolls. Italian sculptors were commissioned to design the heads, while Schoenhut himself perfected the bodies. The spring joints were a great innovation: when a limb of the doll was pulled, the spring was compressed rather than stretched. Even the most destructive child had a fight on his or her hands to pull the heads off these!

Schoenhut dolls have solid carved wooden faces with painted features; the hair is normally either of carved wood or an applied bobbed mohair wig. Although sturdy, the dolls are far from cuddly and make dreadful squeaking noises as their springs are stretched. The problem for modern collectors is that the heavy enamel paint used to paint the dolls' faces has a tendency to crack, craze, and split with age, which can look most unattractive. However, as the firm was forced into bankruptcy during the Depression of the 1930s, their production run was a fairly short one. Today the dolls are rare, highly prized, collector's pieces.

PAPIER-MACHE, COMPOSITION, AND WAXED COMPOSITION DOLLS

THESE WERE SOME OF THE MOST WIDELY USED DOLL-MAKING MATERIALS IN THE EARLY TO LATE NINETEENTH CENTURY. ALTHOUGH GENERALLY LESS SOUGHT-AFTER THAN BISQUE DOLLS, THEY POSSESS AN UNRIVALLED GENTLENESS AND CHARM.

Papier-mâché and composition are two words for essentially the same material, albeit made from differing quantities of similar ingredients. Both are a mixture of paper, wood pulp, glue, and sometimes plaster of Paris (the latter for extra strength). Dolls' heads from the 1830s to 1850s tend to have a high paper-strip content and are called papier-mâché, while the heads of dolls from the 1880s comprise a more compounded mixture of the above-mentioned ingredients and are known as composition.

Papier-mâché became the leading material for dolls' heads from about 1830, but there is evidence to

*A good Biedermeier papier-mâché doll (**above left**), German, c. 1820, with elaborate moulded coiffure, in original printed cotton dress.*
20in (51cm)
£3190 ($5040), Sotheby's London 1989

Two shoulder papier-mâché dolls, French, c. 1840–1850, each with inserted bamboo teeth, on gusseted kid leather bodies.
24in (61cm) and 30in (76cm)
£770 ($1215) and £715 ($1130), Sotheby's London 1989

suggest that papier-mâché dolls were also produced on a commercial basis in the late seventeenth and early eighteenth centuries. The Cockerell family, which originally owned the fine wooden dolls known as Lord and Lady Clapham (described in detail in the first chapter), also possessed a pair of William and Mary papier-mâché dolls, c.1690. The heads and bodies are of papier-mâché, with wooden legs, cloth upper arms and hands of carved wood. Only the heads and shoulder plates are painted and the faces are naïvely rendered with blue eyes and rosebud mouths. They have an altogether gentler appearance than the wooden dolls produced at the same time. It has been suggested that because the hands of these dolls are so similar to those of Lord and Lady Clapham, and because they also wear the same elaborate fontange headdresses, they probably came from the same workshop. This is a tempting attribution to make, but I feel an unlikely one, for several reasons. The facial characteristics are strikingly different; similar wooden hands are found on many wooden dolls of this and later periods; and the fontange was a popular head-dress in common use at the turn of the seventeenth century and so cannot in any way be linked to one particular doll workshop.

Papier-mâché dolls were not produced again in any substantial numbers until the 1830s. During that decade women's fashions in Europe were becoming more and more elaborate. Possibly as a reaction against the slender pinhead look of the Regency period, women's dresses were sprouting angles in every conceivable direction and their hairstyles became burgeoning plaited structures. Woodcarvers found these styles difficult and costly to imitate and began looking around for other, more suitable mediums. Papier-mâché was the perfect solution. This mixture of paper and glue could be pressed into moulds to produce the most elaborate coiffure effects.

In the early 1800s a German sculptor called Friedrich Müller learned the skills of working with papier-mâché from an unknown Frenchman. He and his brother used these skills to great effect in Sonneberg, Thüringia, where they produced various fancy goods, such as trays and mirrors, before expanding their output to include dolls. Thüringia had a well-established doll-making industry and so it would have been an easy step for them to progress to doll-making, incorporating the newly perfected techniques while using the skilled local labour force. Papier-mâché had the advantage of being lighter to transport and therefore such dolls were cheaper to export than wooden ones, presenting an attractive commercial challenge. By 1820 the Müllers had perfected the technique of producing sulphur moulds, into which, first, a layer of petroleum was brushed. Then the paper-pulp mixture (comprising white sand, strips of paper, and animal glue) was pressed into the moulds by hand. Moulds were produced for the front and back of dolls'

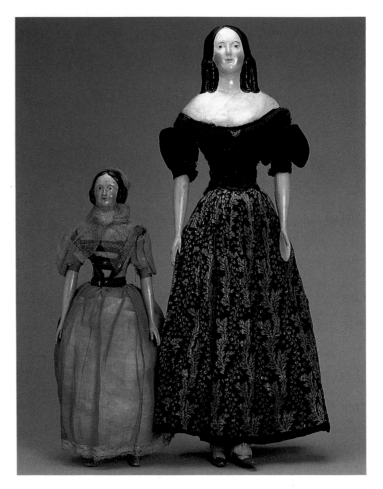

A shoulder papier-mâché doll, German, c. 1840, and another with moulded ringlets c. 1840–1850, both on fabric bodies with wooden lower limbs.
12½in (32cm) and 19in (48cm)
£462 ($730) and £550 ($870), Sotheby's London 1989

heads; the two papier-mâché shells were jointed together, any rough edges removed, and the head then painted and or waxed. These dolls are now known by the collective term of 'Biedermeier dolls', as they were produced in huge numbers in Germany during the 1820s and 1830s, during the Biedermeier period.

Papier-mâché dolls were always produced as shoulder-heads, meaning the heads and shoulder-plates made up one piece. The painted hair colour is almost universally black, and the eyes are painted black or brown. A few male dolls were produced with moulded whiskers, but these are very rare. The shoulder plates are normally glued onto either fabric or kid leather bodies. The arms are either of turned wood or of leather with separately stitched fingers. Unlike the Grödnertal dolls, they are not well articulated and the bodies usually have long, stiff legs without any knee joints. The large clover-shaped hairstyles of the 1830s (with bangs of hair at the top and sides of the head) give way to the long ringlets of the 1840s. The more elaborate the moulded hairstyle of these dolls, the more valuable they are. The waistline of

An important William and Mary papier-mâché and wooden doll, English, c. 1690, with papier-mâché body and wooden legs jointed at hip and knee by means of metal nails and hooks to enable the doll to sit or stand, cloth upper arms and wooden forked hands, painted face, mohair wig, spotted silk open robe and muslin fontange.
17in (43cm)
£9900 ($15640), Sotheby's London 1989

A Motschmann china doll **(right)**, *German c. 1850, with bald head and painted blue eyes, brush-stroked hair, head swivelling on china shoulder-plate, arms and legs of cloth and china jointed at wrists and ankles, china hips and cloth waist.*
10in (25cm)
£1210 ($1910), Sotheby's London 1989

A good waxed papier-mâché Motschmann doll **(far right)**, *German, c. 1850, with jointed papier-mâché and cloth body inserted with squeaker.*
15in (38cm)
£715 ($1130), Sotheby's London 1989

dresses moved from just below the bustline in the 1830s to the more natural waist level of the next decade. The hair and dress of these dolls should therefore be a good guide to dating your own dolls. The Biedermeier style of papier-mâché doll remained popular until the mid-1850s without any real constructional alterations, just changes in dress, hairstyle, and body shape. The 1840s and '50s Biedermeiers are fuller-bosomed and -hipped, with narrow waists.

In the 1840s the French produced their own version of the papier-mâché doll. These are distinguished by their inserted glass eyes and open mouths, which reveal rows of tiny bamboo or ivory teeth. They have highly varnished faces and applied real-hair wigs and although they are unattractive by today's standards, they make an interesting addition to doll collections.

In the 1850s an altogether new style of doll began to be produced in Germany, one which owed a great deal in its design to traditional Japanese dolls. These dolls are known as either Motschmann or Lindner dolls, after the two German doll manufacturers who both claimed to have invented it. In 1851 Edmund Lindner of Sonneberg discovered a Japanese infant doll in a toy shop when he stopped in Cologne on his return trip from the Great Exhibition in London. Until this point the majority of dolls produced had been in the form of women and, to a lesser extent, men. A baby doll was a totally new concept, and one that Lindner thought would be a commercial success.

Hence the 'Sonneberg Baby Doll' was born. In 1857 Charles Motschmann attended the Paris Exposition and also saw the Japanese baby dolls for the first time. He patented his own version in 1857.

Lindner and Motschmann dolls are very similar in design. They consist of papier-mâché, waxed papier-mâché, or porcelain shoulder-heads to which turned wooden lower arms and hands (ball-jointed at the wrist) are attached by strips of fabric. The waist section is concertinaed, made of either fabric or white kid and fitted with a squeaker voice box. The lower torso and tops of the legs are made of papier-mâché, with another tube of kid or leather forming the upper leg, the lower legs and feet of turned wood. The whole is linked together by a system of wires. The heads were bald, often with a few painted curls at the temples reminiscent of the Japanese dolls from which they were copied. Dark enamelled, irisless eyes stare out from the eye slits that were made in the head. With their fully jointed movable bodies, these baby dolls, which were often dressed in a simple shift, marked a radical transition in the development of dolls.

In England in the 1840s, a waxed papier-mâché doll was produced that began to rival the sales of the German Biedermeiers; this is classified by modern collectors as a Slit Head doll. Slit Heads are reminiscent of early nineteenth-century English wooden dolls, with their naïvely sculpted features and irisless enamelled glass eyes. The doll was produced as a shoulder-

Three shoulder papier-mâché dolls (left), German, c. 1840, late 1830s and 1835, with painted faces and moulded hair. 16in (41cm), 17in (43cm) and 15½in (39cm). £2600 ($4110), £800 ($1265) and £1100 ($1740), Sotheby's London 1989 A wax and wood doll (below left), German, c. 1840, with peg jointed wooden body, 13½in (34cm) £1100 ($1740), Sotheby's London 1989. A waxed shoulder papier-mâché doll (below middle), English, early nineteenth century, with cloth body and kid forearms. 14in (36cm) £240 ($380), Sotheby's London 1989. A poured wax shoulder doll (below right), English, c. 1810, with cloth body. 12in (30.5cm) £220 ($350), Sotheby's London 1989

head in papier-mâché and given extra strength by the addition of plaster of Paris to the inner shell. Once the face had been painted the whole thing was dipped into wax to impart a natural-looking complexion. The (human) hair was inserted into a central slit running like a centre-parting from front to back of the doll's head and curled into ringlets at the sides—hence the name Slit Head. The bodies are cheap fabric ones with lower arms of stitched kid in pink, blue, or tan. Some of the dolls have sleeping eyes, which are opened and closed by means of pulling a wire, and their bodies are sometimes fitted with simple squeakers in the middle of the torso. They are often found mounted into shadow boxes and surrounded by fabric or shell flowers, baby shoes, small trinkets, or coloured scraps. The dolls wear inexpensive commercially produced starched muslin gauze gowns, or beautifully crafted handmade gowns. There seems to be no real reason

behind the making of these rather eccentric displays, except that the boxes were probably a craze at that particular time, most likely promoted by popular ladies' handicraft papers.

By the 1860s the dolls with ringlets disappeared and in their place came the Pumpkin Head. These are generally believed to have been made in Germany, but some examples could certainly have been made in England as the facial characteristics resemble those of other English models. The name Pumpkin Head derives from the similarity between the round hollow-sounding vegetable and the doll's hollow, moulded, yellow-painted head. Pumpkin Heads have moulded short blonde hairstyles and sometimes coloured bonnets as well (those with bonnets are highly desirable). The arms and legs are of simple turned wood, with ankle boots often painted onto the feet in a jaunty Bavarian style.

By the 1870s dolls were again popularly produced in the form of lady dolls and a striving for realism in their design and manufacture was evident once more. Fine dolls of parian (unglazed porcelain) and bisque (matte-glazed porcelain) were in great demand. Dolls made of waxed composition were a cheaper alternative and were produced in large numbers in Germany and France. Both are similar in construction, being shoulder-heads with composition lower limbs. The only way of telling the two countries' products apart are by their eyes. The French dolls have the deep paperweight eyes found on their bisque dolls, whereas the German dolls' eyes, although of spun glass, do not have the same realistic depth. These dolls often have elaborate mohair wigs piled high on the head and, once again, blonde hair is more fashionable. The bodies are fabric and the lower legs are often modelled with exquisite tasselled ankle boots. These later dolls tend to have very pink complexions, a trait that is not always attractive. The dresses are often elaborate, of brightly coloured satins. Wired eyes have been abandoned and fixed eyes are the order of the day, although a very small number have the weighted sleeping eyes that were beginning to be used in the more expensive bisque versions. Although inexpensive in comparison to the bisque dolls made at the same date they are marvellous fashion records, with the gowns in which they are dressed and their elaborate hairstyles testifying to the tastes of the time in which they were created.

The demand for child dolls, or 'Bébés', grew in the 1880s, and unwaxed composition dolls were made to imitate the fine French bisque dolls being produced by manufacturers like Emile Jumeau. These are mainly of waxed composition, have painted pink complexions, heavily painted eyebrows and long lashes, and large round paperweight eyes. The heads are often applied with short curly goatskin wigs to imitate infant curls. Because they cannot be attributed to any particular manufacturer, and because if rubbed the complexions are irreversibly damaged, they command very low

A split head doll, English, c. 1845, with blonde wig, black enamelled eyes, fabric body with kid lower arms.

A waxed composition lady doll, German, 1875–1880, with fabric body and waxed composition lower limbs, head turned slightly to one side, inset blue glass eyes, blonde mohair wig and original clothing of highly decorated satin ball gown.
Münchner Stadtmuseum

prices in the salerooms (unlike their bisque counterparts, which they imitate).

Composition was used by bisque doll manufacturers up until the 1930s as a cheaper alternative to porcelain. After this date celluloid and other plastics became more prevalent. Composition dolls can be found bearing almost identical mould numbers and markings as the bisque dolls that they copy. Armand Marseille, the Heubach brothers, S.F.B.J. (Société Française de Fabrication des Bébés et Jouets), and Heinrich Handwerk all produced dolls in composition. As collectors tend to concentrate on bisque dolls, composition dolls are very inexpensive and therefore make a good starting-off point for the new doll collector with a limited budget.

The drawback to collecting these papier-mâché-based dolls is that they tend to suffer from cracking and splitting. The cracks often run from the shoulder plate and up into the head. If the cracks are limited to the shoulder plate the loss in value will not be too great, as collectors normally expect and accept a little

damage of this kind. However, once the cracks spread to the face and hair the value of a piece drops dramatically. Waxed composition dolls suffer terribly from cracking, the Slit Head examples often sporting a craze of interlocking cracks over the entire surface of the head. Since the majority of Slit Heads are like this, these 'impurities' should be accepted as part of the aging process of this particular kind of doll and not as major defects. The cracks result from the shell and the wax covering expanding and contracting at different rates. Because the dolls are sensitive to temperature and humidity changes, it is not a good idea to store them in centrally heated rooms, nor to frequently move them about from one room to another.

Great care should be taken when examining papier-mâché and composition dolls and any deterioration to the head should be taken into consideration when purchases are being made. Sadly, if the finishing coating of varnish is removed from the heads (often as the result of a child trying to give the doll a wash), very little can be done to restore it successfully.

POURED WAX DOLLS

WAX DOLLS REACHED THEIR PEAK OF EXCELLENCE AND POPULARITY IN THE MIDDLE TO LATE NINETEENTH CENTURY. THEY ARE THE MOST UNSETTLINGLY REALISTIC OF ALL DOLL TYPES, WITH THEIR WARM FLESHY TEXTURE AND FINELY DETAILED FACES.

The golden age for wax doll production was from the mid- to late nineteenth century, and its centre was England. However, the necessary skills were learned from countries such as Italy, Germany, and to a lesser degree France, all of which had long traditions in manufacturing beautifully detailed religious figures. There are surviving examples of fourteenth- and fifteenth-century wax portraits produced in Nuremberg, Cologne, and Augsburg, and the collection of the History Museum in Wroclaw (Breslau), Poland, includes one of Mary Queen of Scots. Numerous Italian portrait and religious reliefs produced from the sixteenth century onwards are housed in London's Victoria and Albert Museum and in most other major international museums, all of which stand as a testament to the high skill and perfection attained by these Italian artisans. In eighteenth-century Paris members of the Clouet family were renowned for their wax reliefs, while in England Thomas Engelhardt submitted wax portraits to the Royal Academy between the years 1773 and 1786. But it is not until the mid-nineteenth century that England became the centre for producing these exquisitely modelled dolls, which were not mere playthings but sculpted works of art in their own right.

The nineteenth-century desire to artificially re-create nature (as reflected in the domes of wax fruit, cases of stuffed birds, and rise in popularity of Madame Tussaud's waxworks), combined with a morbid and sentimental obsession with death, provided a perfect climate for producing realistic sculptures and models in wax, which once more became a popular medium. Wax renditions of the infant Jesus, nestled on a bed of silk flowers and dried grasses and contained within a dome of glass, can look alarmingly sinister to the twentieth-century observer but at the time of their creation they were much admired.

Unlike the other mediums for doll-making, wax is extremely lifelike, realistic, and unlike bisque it is warm to the touch. The colouring of the skin tones can be very true to life, and human hair (often supplied from the child's own locks) was individually inserted into the hot wax to form eyelashes, eyebrows, and

*A fine, rare shoulder wax doll (**above left and right**), probably by Montanari, English, c. 1850. This doll is believed to be a portrait of Princess Alice as a child (born April 1843), in original eau de nil fringed silk outfit. 18in (46cm) £3740 ($5910), Sotheby's London 1989*

sprouting tufts that followed the natural hairline. On the very best quality dolls, the effect is startlingly real.

Wax dolls became popular playthings for the children of the rich around 1840. The two major English doll-makers were the Montanaris and the Pierottis, whose names reveal an Italian heritage. The former family, however, also included a native Englishwoman, Charlotte Augusta Dalton (1818–1864), who married Napoleon Montanari (b.1813), a Corsican-born wax modeller. Their son Richard Napoleon (b.1840), one of four children, carried on the family business of doll-making. The Pierotti doll-making dynasty was started by Domenico Pierotti (b.1760), who emigrated from Italy to England around 1780, marrying English-woman Susanna Sleight 10 years later. He made wax dolls and portraits and in the nineteenth century his son Anericho Cephas (known as Henry) continued the family tradition. Henry is listed in the London Trade Directory of 1847 as a maker of wax and com-

A fine Charles Pierotti poured wax baby doll (above), English, c. 1860, incised C. Pierotti, with fabric body and waxed lower limbs, the head turned slightly to the left with rosebud closed mouth, blue eyes, blonde inserted hair and lace gown.
21in (53cm) £880 ($1540), Sotheby's London 1989

A fine, rare wax doll (right), English, c. 1757, the finely modelled wax head with inset black irisless eyes, real hair wig, dressed in elaborate court robe trimmed with pink furbelows.
15¾in (40cm) Bethnal Green Museum

position figures. His grandchildren carried on the business well into the twentieth century.

Both the Montanari and Pierotti companies exhibited their wares at major European trade exhibitions. Madame Augusta Montanari, as she was known, won a prize medal for her wax dolls at the 1851 Great Exhibition and the report on her stand compiled by the judging committee read as follows:

[The] Display of this Exhibitor is the most remarkable and beautiful collection of toys in the Great Exhibition. It is a series of dolls representing all ages, from infancy to womanhood, arranged in several family groups . . . The dolls have hair, eyelashes and eyelids separately inserted in wax . . . a variety of expressions are given to the figures in regard to the ages and stations which they were intended to represent. The dolls are adapted for children of the wealthy rather than general sale, undressed dolls sell from 10 shillings, dressed dolls are much more expensive.

Madame Montanari also displayed a small number of rag dolls that were aimed at the cheaper end of the market.

Three pressed wax bead eye dolls, English, c. 1840, with fabric bodies and wax lower limbs.
6in (15cm), 7in (18cm) and 4³/4in (12cm)
£352 ($555), £176 ($280) and £264 ($420), Sotheby's London 1989

In the early to mid-nineteenth century wax heads were produced by carving solid blocks of wax. These dolls, made in both Germany and England, are normally small in size with small black beadwork eyes that were simply pushed into the warm wax head. By the 1840s the more expensive poured wax dolls were being produced and the solid wax dolls became scarce. To produce a poured wax doll, hot molten wax—to which a flesh tint had been added—was poured into metal, clay, or wooden moulds; these were allowed to cool slightly and then the excess was poured off, leaving a thin shell of wax. The better-quality dolls were produced by as many as three or four different pourings, each layer of wax building up the flesh tone of the dolls. Some were further strengthened by being given a thin interior layer of plaster of Paris. The next step was the insertion of the eyes. Apertures were cut into the head, and the glass eyes were heated under a gas jet and set in. On the better-quality dolls, eyelids and

*A fine Montanari poured wax shoulder doll, **(above and left)**, English, 1850s, with cloth body and wax lower limbs, finely painted mouth and cheek colouring, blue glass eyes, inserted eyelashes and brown hair.*
13¾in (35cm)
£1650 ($2610), Sotheby's London 1989

eyebrows would then be carefully applied and modelled, and eyelashes and eyebrows inserted. Rouge would be added to the cheeks, and vermilion served to highlight the mouth and nostrils. Another craftsman would then insert the real-hair wigs tuft by tuft into the wax scalp. Some doll-makers advertised that they could insert locks of the child's own hair if so desired. The lower arms and legs would also be made of hollow poured wax; these were stitched onto a simple stuffed white cotton body through special eyelets inserted into the wax pieces.

If the dolls are marked at all (the majority are not), they are stamped (or signed in ink) with the manufacturer's name on the chest of the fabric body. Some Pierotti dolls have the name 'H. Pierotti' incised into the wax on the back of the shoulder plate, but this is very rare. Dolls made by Montanari often have a very high, pink colouring, unlike the more peachy tones of the Pierotti models. The Montanaris tend to have slightly bulging eyes and very prominent rolls of fat at

A fine wax portrait doll of Queen Victoria (**far left**), probably by Montanari, English, c. 1840, with fine modelled head, glass eyes and real hair wig. 22¾in (58cm) Bethnal Green Museum, London

A rare poured wax portrait doll of Queen Victoria (**left**), probably by Montanari, English, c. 1885, with cloth body and wax lower limbs, and well-moulded face with inset blue eyes. 19¼in (49cm) £550 ($865), Sotheby's London 1989

the neck and wrists. The expressions of the Pierottis are softer, the faces less stylized.

The popularity of the British royal family was exploited by the doll-makers (especially the Montanaris), and portrait dolls of Queen Victoria and her children were produced. Beautiful and flattering portrait waxes of the young monarch survive, as do the more curious figures of Her Majesty as a rather dumpy old lady complete with grey hair and wrinkles. It is hard to imagine any child clasping this piece to her bosom with any affection whatsoever, and one can only assume that they were produced to satisfy patriotic adults!

Other major English wax doll-makers to look out for are Charles Marsh (1865–1913), who not only made but repaired and cleaned wax dolls; Mrs Lucy Peck (1891–1921) of The Doll's Home, 131 Regent Street;

H. J. Meech (1865–1891) of 50 Kennington Road, London, who was doll-maker to the royal family by special appointment; and W.H. Cremer & Son, whose first shop was in Bond Street and who later moved to Regent Street.

Wax dolls were at their most popular around 1860 but became less so as the century progressed. Although they were wonderfully realistic, they were also fragile and very expensive, and needed careful handling. They were easily cracked and broken, and in addition to this they melted. Sturdier and cheaper waxed composition dolls became popular in the 1870s, as did the bisque and parian lady dolls produced with great finesse in France and Germany. The quality of wax dolls degenerated towards the end of the century, with the exception of those made by Pierotti and Mrs Peck, who produced fine dolls into the early 1900s.

GLAZED CHINA AND PARIAN DOLLS

HEADS WITH BRIGHTLY COLOURED GLAZED FACES, HAIRSTYLES AND ORNAMENTS WERE PRODUCED IN LARGE NUMBERS FROM THE 1840s ONWARDS, PREDOMINANTLY BY GERMAN AND FRENCH PORCELAIN FACTORIES. THEY APPEAL TO BOTH DOLL AND PORCELAIN COLLECTORS ALIKE.

Porcelain dolls fall into three doll-collecting categories: glazed china, parian, and bisque. It is useful to understand the differences between them, since they are often confused. All porcelain dolls are made from hard-paste porcelain, which is a mixture of ground white kaolin stone (china clay) and petuntse (china stone). The differences lie within the firing and glazing methods. Large quantities of kaolin were found around Sèvres in France and Berlin, Meissen, and the summer palace at Nymphenburg in Germany, so it was natural that major porcelain factories were soon established in these areas. Many of these made doll's heads in addition to the more common items of domestic porcelain, and although prestigious factories like Meissen are believed to have produced doll's heads, no marked examples seem to be in existence any longer.

Dolls' heads of parian and bisque are basically the same. Sometimes incorrectly described as matte-glazed porcelain, bisque is in fact fired unglazed porcelain, as is parian, the name taken from a type of white marble (originating on the Greek island of Paros). From 1846 the English porcelain company Copeland & Garret (later W.T. Copeland & Sons) used 'Parian' as a trade name for its refined, creamy-textured hard paste porcelain which, upon firing, looked like the marble. At some point in the intervening years doll collectors adopted the name 'parian' to refer to white-complexioned, unglazed shoulder-bisque dolls. A porcelain collector would argue that to be parian a piece would need to be an English-produced hard-paste porcelain object, preferably by the firm of Copeland. However, misnomer or not, they will continue to be called parian dolls. The only real difference between dolls termed parian and those called bisque

*A shoulder parian doll (**above left, left**), German, c. 1850, and a Simon & Halbig shoulder parian doll (**above left, right**), German, c. 1860.*
11½in (29cm) and 16in (41cm)
£520 ($820) and £780 ($1230), Sotheby's London 1989

is that a coloured pigment was added to the clay on the bisques to give a pinky flesh-complexioned tint before firing.

China dolls became popular in the 1840s. To make them, the clay was either pressed or poured into two moulds, the resultant pair then being joined together and fired to produce a single biscuit or bisque piece. It was then dipped in clear, shiny glaze and fired again. Next, the facial characteristics and hair colouring were applied with coloured enamels, and the piece was then given a third firing to fix the paint. The vari-

Two glazed china Bathing Children (frozen Charlies or Charlottes) dolls (left), German, c. 1860, one with glazed blonde hair, the other dark.
15¹/₂in (39cm)
Münchner Stadtmuseum

A shoulder parian (above left, left), German, c. 1860, and a Simon & Halbig shoulder parian doll (above left, right), German, c. 1870. 11¹/₂in (29cm) and 16in (41cm) £520 ($820) and £780 ($1230), Sotheby's London 1989

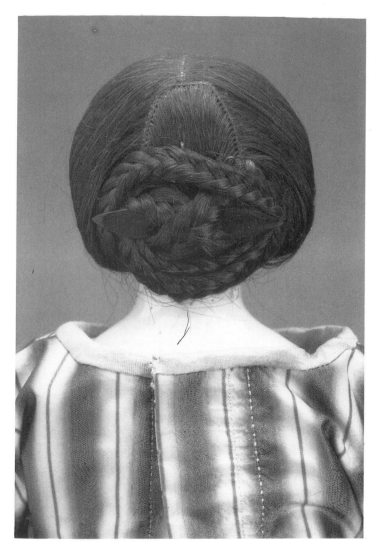

A good shoulder china doll, German, c. 1840, with cloth body and stitched joints and kid arms, glazed features, applied auburn wig in elaborate braided hairstyle – the braids held in place by a tortoiseshell pin, painted black

domed head and original purple striped dress. 17¼in (44cm) £990 ($1555), Sotheby's London 1989

coloured enamels required firing at different temperatures—for example, blues, purples and blacks at a much higher temperature than yellow—and this fact might explain why so many of the dolls produced in the 1840s and '50s have dark brown or black hair, as the face and hair glazes could be achieved in a single firing. An exception to this general rule was the Meissen factory, which developed its own range of coloured enamels, all of which could be fired at roughly the same temperature.

Germany was the major country for producing glazed china dolls from the 1840s. Those with moulded ringlets or buns normally have glazed black hair (in rare cases they have dark brown hair). Dolls with dark brown glazed hairstyles are more valuable than black-haired models. Some dolls of the 1840s are produced with circular black glazed areas a bit like skullcaps. These were meant to have applied real-hair wigs—usually of human hair, elaborately plaited and coiled—

which were pasted on. The more elaborate and beautiful the hairstyle, the more valuable the doll. Indeed, the hairstyles are the main interest in these dolls as the painted features of their faces are fairly pedestrian and do not differ enormously from doll to doll. The shoulder-heads are mounted onto simple gusseted fabric bodies with glazed china lower limbs.

China dolls and parian dolls were produced from the 1850s in very similar styles. The construction and decoration of the dolls were identical, except that china dolls had a shiny glaze and parians did not. From the 1850s to '60s, there was a general craze for baby dolls, so inevitably all-china baby dolls began to appear. These are known as Frozen Charlies or, if they have obviously female hairstyles, Frozen Charlottes. Hairstyles are the only means of telling the sexes apart, since Victorian standards of prudery dictated that all dolls have exactly the same androgynous bodies. They are totally rigid, without any moving joints, and come

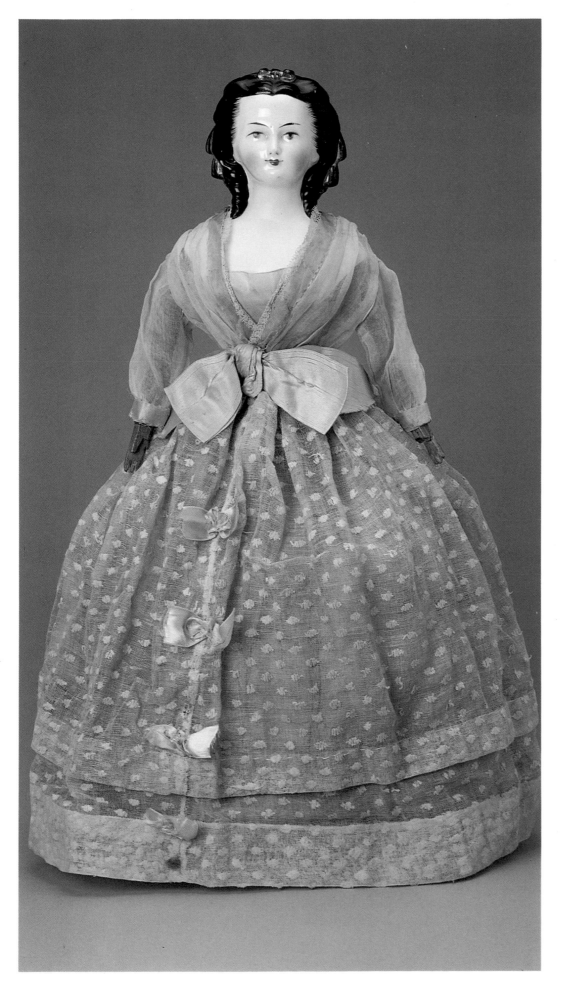

A fine glazed china
shoulder doll, **(left)**,
German, c. 1850,
with enamelled coloured
head, glazed lustred bow
and gilded snood to the
hair and original white
voile dress.
17in (43cm)
£990 ($1565), Sotheby's
London 1989

Two Madame Rohmer glazed china swivel-head dolls, French, c. 1860, both bearing blue oval Rohmer stamps to kid leather bodies, the one on the left in original printed muslin costume and the one on the right re-dressed. 13¾in (35cm) and 14in (36cm) £2640 ($4170) and £1870 ($2955), Sotheby's London 1989

in a variety of sizes, from about 1in (2.5cm)—useful for burying in Christmas puddings—to 18in (46cm).

From the late 1860s up to the 1870s lady dolls were once again in vogue, and the hairstyles and hair adornments of dolls became one of their salient features. The hair is commonly blonde, instead of the uniform black of the 1840s. This change in hair colour probably reflected not only the fashion of the time, but also the technological advances in producing enamel colours, which meant that they could all be fixed in one firing. More colours are used and more decorations adorn the heads. Pink and blue feathers, gilded snoods, and flowers bedeck the hair, and multicoloured and 'gem'-inset necklaces and ribbon chokers appear on the necks. Dolls with very elaborate snoods are often referred to as Princess Eugénie dolls.

By 1870 swivel-head dolls were beginning to appear in large numbers. Unlike the shoulder-head dolls those with swivel necks (where the neck swivels and rotates in

a neck socket in the separately made shoulder plate) could turn their heads. Another development was that glass eyes began to be inserted into the glazed china, bisque, and parian heads, which made the dolls look more realistic. Glazed china and parian dolls were still produced in the early to mid-1870s, but after this bisque dolls predominated.

In Germany in the late 1860s and early 1870s, the Simon & Halbig porcelain company produced swivel-necked parian dolls with moulded blonde hair, inset fixed eyes of blue glass, heavily outlined in black, bearing the initial 'S' or 'SH' and a number impressed onto the front base of the shoulder plate, attached to simple fabric bodies. In Paris Mlle Marie Antoinette Rohmer (*fl.*1857–80) and the Maison Huret (1850–1920), under the direction of Mlle Calixte Huret, were both producing exquisite glazed and bisque swivel-necked dolls, the earlier ones having painted eyes, those of the mid- to late 1870s featuring inset glass

eyes. Both these French dolls have the well-articulated kid-leather or kid-covered wood bodies that were to make the French dolls so popular. When marked these dolls bear ink stamps on the kid leather of the chests. The French dolls not only had better bodies but were equipped with superb outfits of clothes and accessories. Both these factors were to make French dolls the most expensive and sought after between 1870 and 1890.

Cheap glazed china dolls were produced in ever-decreasing quality up until 1914. The later dolls have white faces and simple black bobbed hairstyles, and are often small in size for use in doll houses.

Glazed porcelain dolls enjoyed a brief return to popularity between 1900 and 1920, when half-dolls, or pincushion dolls, were produced in both Germany and France. Rather than playthings for children, they were intended as an adult indulgence and decorated the boudoirs and dressing tables of women. Those produced around 1900 copy the eighteenth-century Meissen style of figure, i.e. elegant ladies with elaborate glazed hairstyles and delicately modelled hands and arms. By the late 1920s these were still produced in

A selection of 17 china and bisque half dolls, German twentieth century, the smallest 3¼in (8.25cm) and the largest 10¾in (27.5cm) including skirt.
£275 to £462 ($510 to $860), Sotheby's London 1988

the romantic eighteenth-century style, but they also appeared in a chic Art Deco flapper mode. Generally speaking, however, as time passed the quality of these dolls worsened—until cheap, poorly moulded and sloppily glazed 'crinolined' ladies adorned pincushions and powder pots.

BISQUE DOLLS

DELICATE AND FULL OF CHARACTER

WITHOUT BEING ROUGH OR RUGGED,

IT IS NOT SURPRISING THAT THIS

IS ONE OF THE MOST POPULAR AND

SOUGHT-AFTER OF ALL DOLL TYPES,

FEATURING PROMINENTLY IN

THE 'GOLDEN AGE' OF THE DOLL-

MAKER'S ART.

Another type of doll with special appeal to collectors is that made of bisque, a fired clay that may or may not have been tinted and has not been given a finishing glaze. The two principal manufacturers of bisque dolls were France and Germany, although other countries attempted production as well, for instance, during World War I, when the political and economic climate made their importation impossible. However, British dolls were poor-quality, clumsy, and unconvincing copies, and although they possessed a naïve charm, they did not compare with the French and German dolls they aimed to replace. The British porcelain manufacturers were more at home and adept at producing china dinner services and other domestic ware —unlike the German firms, some of which had well over a century of experience and expertise in the manufacture of dolls.

At first, the heads of bisque dolls were produced by ceramics factories that had been commissioned by the various doll manufacturers; the various other constituents of the dolls were made by outworkers and then assembled and marketed by the doll-maker in the final stage. By the late nineteenth century, factories had been set up in both Germany and France that situated all the required component-making skills and equipment under one roof or in one complex. Specialists included the mould-makers, clay preparers, wig- and eye-makers, painters, and costume-makers.

The early bisque dolls, those pre-1890, were usually made by the pressed clay method, with the faster and more economical poured clay method becoming more popular in the latter part of the century. With the

A fine, rare Huret shoulder bisque doll, French, c. 1865, stamped in blue on the chest MAISON HURET, Boulevard 22, PARIS, and circular stamp 6 EXPOSITION UNIVERSAL DE 1865, with composition body and ball joints to the hips, knees and arms, painted blue eyes, chubby cheeks, black mohair wig over cork pate, original outfit with hooped crinoline and leather boots.
16in (41cm)
£5720 ($9040), Sotheby's London 1989

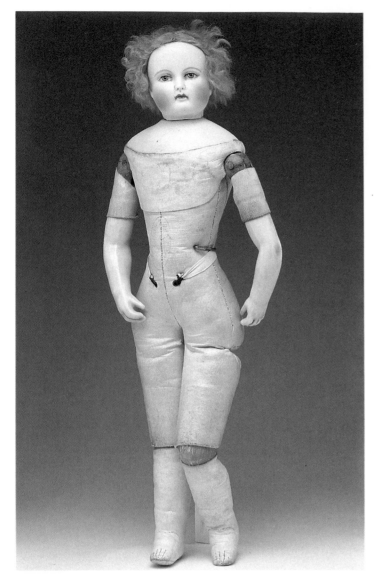

*A fine Madame Rohmer bisque doll (**above and left**), French, c. 1850, undressed to show body construction, complete with trunk of original costume, including bonnets, shoes, skirts, dresses, parasols and coats. 16in (41cm) £17600 ($27810), Sotheby's London 1989*

earlier pressed clay technique, the ceramics factory would leave the kaolin (porcelain clay) mixture to macerate in water—the longer it was left, the better the resultant clay. The water was drained off, and the dough-like clay was kneaded and rolled between cylinders before being cut into squares. These squares were sized to correspond with the two-part, plaster-cast moulds into which they were carefully pressed in place by hand. After the heads had dried out enough to retain their shape, they were removed from the moulds, eye and mouth apertures were cut, the two halves were joined, and the separately moulded ears were applied. The heads were next placed with their crowns down onto trays and fired in very hot kilns for between twenty-seven and forty-eight hours. After cooling they were polished with sandpaper, and mineral pigments were applied to give the pink flesh colour. The cheeks, lips, nostrils, eyebrows, and eye-lashes were then completed before a second firing of about seven hours at a much lower temperature, which ensured their permanence. When examining a pressed clay doll you will notice that the head is thicker and rougher on the inside, which should aid you in dating

it. Where ears have been applied you will see a fine line running around the perimeter of the ear: this is due to the clay separating slightly from the head during firing.

The poured clay heads required a very fine aqueous clay mixture, which meant that the clay mixture had to be drawn through a number of increasingly fine sieves. It was then poured into the moulds and excess drained off, prior to drying, firing, filing off the mould lines, and finishing in the manner described above. With larger heads, the ears would still need to be applied, whereas smaller heads would have the ears included in the basic mould.

In the 1860s and 1870s the use of porcelain for dolls' heads had become both popular and common-place. From the 1870s to the early 1890s, it was the turn of the French to become pre-eminent in the doll-making world. This is regarded as the 'Golden Age' of doll manufacture, as the French producers turned a humble plaything into a work of art that was to rival any doll produced before or since.

FRENCH BISQUE DOLLS

The first intrinsically French doll to emerge in the 1870s was the swivel-head, or socket-head, doll. This type of doll was patented by Mademoiselle Huret as

A fine swivel-head bisque fashion doll (above), French, c. 1870, unmarked, with gusseted kid leather body with separately stitched fingers, in original costume and complete with trunk of further outfits and accessories.
16in (41cm) £4730 ($7425), Sotheby's London 1989
The head of a fine Bru fashion doll (left), French, c. 1875, the head and shoulder impressed K, with kid body.
25in (64cm) £5500 ($8960), Sotheby's London 1989

early as 1861, but it was not until the 1870s that it became a commonplace. Although there were numerous small factories in Paris making swivel-heads by that decade, the main producers were Casimir Bru, Emile Jumeau, François Gaultier, Maison Huret, Maison Rohmer, and F. Simonne. Made as lady dolls, these swivel-heads are also referred to as Parisiennes, after the city where the majority of them were produced, or Fashion dolls, as the costumes in which they were attired were sumptuous—and accurate—miniature renditions of leading dress styles.

The name swivel-head derives from the arrangement of a head and neck moulded in one section that fits into a shoulder plate with a neck socket, in which the head can be more realistically turned and posed.

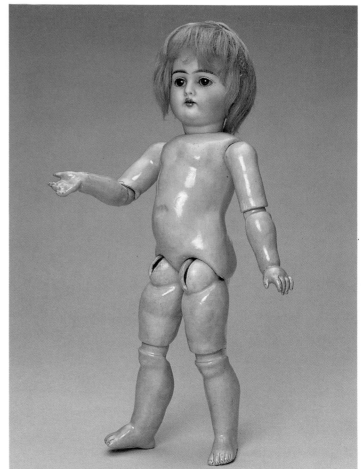

A Bru Jeune body with gusseted leather limbs and bisque shoulder plate, French, 1875–1885.
Sotheby's London

A Kämmer & Reinhardt wood and composition toddler body with well-moulded torso, German, c. 1900.
Sotheby's London

Most other dolls—be they wax, china, or composition —were produced as shoulder-heads, whose head and shoulders were made as one immovable piece. On swivel-head dolls you will often find an impressed maker's mark to the sides at the very base of the shoulder plate, slightly concealed below the edging of the kid body. The bodies could be of inexpensive calico with wired limbs, the sort found on, for example, a cheap Breton fisherwoman doll of the souvenir type. The better quality, medium-range dolls had bodies of gusseted white kid with prominent hips and bottoms, these shaped to give the voluptuous curves that were the order of the day, and for further realism their fingers and toes were often individually stitched. Some of these Parisiennes will have ink-stamps on their chests bearing the name and trading address of the manufacturer. It is therefore a good idea to check this area on a doll if no maker's mark can be located on the shoulder plate (assuming of course that the doll can be undressed without doing any harm to the costume).

The gusseted kid-leather body is the standard type, but others were produced with bodies capable of in-

credible movement. The firms of Jumeau, Bru, and Huret are known to have experimented with and patented designs for wooden bodies covered with gutta-percha, in an attempt to achieve a cheaper alternative to leather. Jumeau produced a wooden articulated body, bisque shoulder plate with moulded bosoms, and bisque lower limbs with moulded ankle boots. Others were of wood with ball-jointed limbs, the whole covered in pink stockinette or kid (known as Gesland types) or of finely polished wood finished off with a layer of pink paint. These normally have bisque lower arms for added beauty. Maison Huret is also known to have produced dolls with painted metal hands. Of course, dolls with unusual, high-quality bodies are extremely rare and normally fetch twice as much as those with the standard kid bodies.

Although Maison Huret dolls were produced with both painted and glass eyes, the majority of swivel-heads were made with pale blue, spiralled-glass eyes. These dolls have creamy-complexioned, slightly chubby faces. The Jumeau dolls were sometimes incised with the initials 'E.J.', but more commonly they were left unmarked. The unmarked dolls can some-

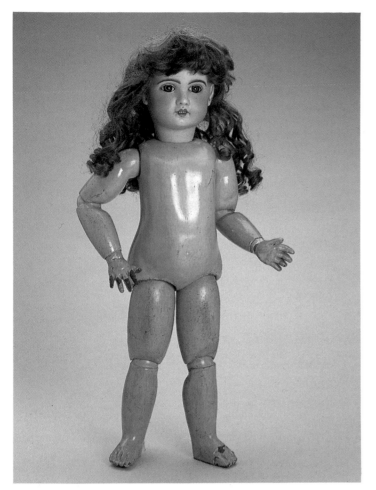

A Jumeau turned wood and composition chunky toddler body, French, c. 1890.
Sotheby's London

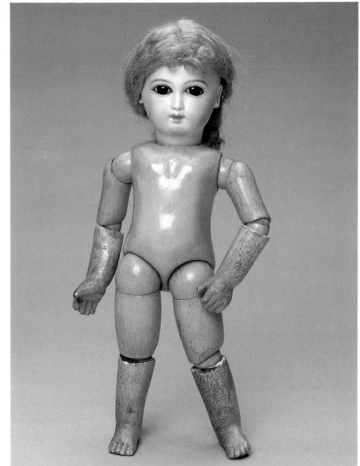

An early Jumeau body, French, c. 1870, with eight floating ball joints, straight wrists and composition torso.
Sotheby's London

times be attributed to Jumeau, however, by the marvellous quality blue eyes that have been used. Jumeau dolls were famous for their deep, paperweight eyes made from rods of spiralled glass, which give an impression of great depth and realism. Dolls made by Bru are incised with a variety of the lower range of alphabet letters, including A, B, C, or K. In addition the identity of a Bru can sometimes be confirmed if the doll possesses a sweetly smiling mouth. The Simonne dolls are often of a very white bisque and appear to have fatter faces and arms. The Gaultier dolls are usually well marked, with the initials 'F. G.' placed above the arms on the shoulder plate.

All these lady dolls were produced with pierced ears to take pendant earrings and hair wigs that were applied to cork pates. The use of cork pates meant that the high-quality glass eyes could easily be inserted by the workmen into the head and that any repairs required could be carried out at a later date. It also provided a suitable base on which to apply the increasingly elaborate coiffures. The hair used for the wig was sometimes that of the Tibetan goat, although more commonly it was of mohair. The more expensive dolls sported human hair, this having been provided by poor women who could exchange their crowning glories for much-needed cash (see *Little Women* by Louisa May Alcott for an example of this). When home-grown supplies of hair became scarce, the Chinese were persuaded to chop off their pigtails and sell them as well. Although the fashion at the time was predominantly for blonde or Titian red, the raven Oriental locks would simply be bleached and then dyed any desired shade.

If you are lucky enough to acquire a bisque doll in its original, elaborate silk costume, then you have in your possession a swivel-head that can quite rightly be called a Fashion doll. Some of these were accompanied by trunks full of alternative gowns, as frequent changes of dress (at this date between four and six changes of outfit a day!) were normal for the middle and upper classes. Everything required for the grand lady was produced in miniature for the dolls. In Paris, the Passage de Choiseul was the centre of this industry, with its workshops producing tiny ankle boots, wigs, corsets, bonnets, tortoiseshell dressing sets, scent bottles, fans, opera glasses, and even miniature silver

JUMEAU
MEDAILLE D'OR
PARIS

DÉPOSÉ
E.7J.

DÉPOSÉ
TETE JUMEAU
B^{TE} SGDG
6

A selection of marks found on Jumeau dolls. 'Jumeau Medaille d'Or Paris' is a body stamp and the other two are head stamps.

tea sets. Sadly, many of the dolls' splendid costumes were produced by exploited Parisian outworkers, skilled seamstresses who toiled in unsuitable and impoverished conditions for very little reward.

Modern collectors are incredulous that these beautiful dolls in their magnificent costumes were produced and intended ostensibly as playthings and so search for another explanation to their purpose. It has been suggested that Fashion dolls were dressed by couturiers and sent out to all parts of the globe as ambassadors of fashion, and as a means of showing women how to correctly assemble all the constituent parts needed to make the dress appear as intended. I think this highly unlikely, as a ladies' fashion journal would do the same job at a lower cost. A more likely explanation might be that some dolls were dressed in the fashion of the day and placed in dressmakers' windows

A fine, rare Jumeau portrait bisque doll (above), French, c. 1875, the pale head impressed 1, with early eight-ball jointed wood and composition body, fixed almond-shaped brown paperweight eyes, remains of sheepskin wig, original blue satin dress, bonnet and leather boots.
11in (28cm) Sotheby's London 1990
An Emile Jumeau bisque doll (right), French c. 1880, impressed 'Depose E.6.J', with jointed composition body and straight wrists, blue stamp on buttocks, closed mouth, fixed blue glass paperweight eyes, blonde wig and original maroon satin dress.
14½in (37cm) £4400 ($7700), Sotheby's London 1988

simply because full-sized outfits demonstrating the current fashions, fabrics, and trimmings available would take up too much shop space.

The majority of these splendidly attired dolls *were*

intended for children, however, and not just as retailers' advertisements. By the 1870s the child's nursery was equipped with rocking horses and toys of every description, and was as much a vehicle for showing off one's wealth as the more obvious forms of houses, carriages, jewellery, and clothes. The uncomfortably overdressed Parisiennes perfectly reflect the time in which they were made, when wealthy women were adorned from head to toe and were expected not to work but to be ornamental companions to their husbands. The pampered children for whom the dolls were intended would be waited upon by a large staff of servants, and a nanny saw to it that play was strictly supervised and nothing broken.

By the 1880s the fashion for the lady doll had waned and the Bébé was born. Little girls to a large degree had tired of playing with miniature versions of their mothers (although Jumeau still produced Parisiennes until the late 1890s on special commission), and they now wanted well-dressed little versions of themselves. The Bébés are intended to represent a preadolescent child, sometimes a toddler of three or four, sometimes a more grown-up, long-haired version intended to be around ten years old. The early Bébés of the late 1870s–early 1880s have interesting bodies, their limbs of lathe-turned, floating ball-jointed wood with a papier-mâché torso. In line with the Parisiennes, the early heads have paler, almost white complexions, but they also have huge spiralled glass eyes. These early examples often have wigs of curly kid to imitate infant curls.

Some of these early forms of Bébé bear the incised marks of Emile Jumeau, which probably proves his claim that he was the inventor of this style of doll. However, the French doll-makers were constantly pirating one another's ideas, adopting and adapting new designs as they were conceived, so it is difficult to be certain just who the initiator of the original design was. It must be remembered that Jumeau's claims were not always reliable: he claimed to have invented the swivel-head doll, too, but patent records show that it was actually Mademoiselle Huret.

In the 1890s the poured clay method was more widely adopted for producing the bisque heads of Bébés, and from the 1880s composition was used to form the limbs as well as the bodies (with wood being used as ball joints and upper leg joints, a method that helped reduce the cost of the product). Jumeau, Bru, Steiner, Schmitt and Fils, and Gaultier were the major producers of Bébés. Jumeau and Bru were perhaps the most prolific manufacturers, and today their products are the most desirable of all French dolls.

JUMEAU, THE KING OF DOLLS

Jumeau's contribution to the French doll industry was outstanding. He was the first to produce a bisque doll that was totally French in construction, that was manufactured in a factory environment rather than by outworkers, and his dolls not only competed with the finest German examples,but outshone them.

The first record of a Monsieur Pierre François Jumeau appears in 1842 in the Paris *Almanac de Commerce,* wherein both he and a mysterious Monsieur Belton are listed as makers of kid dolls and dressed dolls at 14 rue Salle au Compte in Paris. At this point their expertise lay in producing the kid-leather bodies and fine outfits of the dolls, whose heads, probably of papier-mâché, were produced elsewhere in France, as well as imported from Germany. In the Paris Exposition of French Industry in 1844 they received an Honourable Mention for their stand. By 1847 the name Belton had disappeared from all records, and from this date until 1867 Pierre Jumeau is listed alone as a doll-maker at 18 rue Mauconseil, Paris. His astute attempts to bring his dolls to the attention of a wider public and to gain foreign exports led him to exhibit his wares at most of the major international trade fairs, all of which brought him great acclaim and increased order books. In 1849 in Paris he won a bronze medal, and in the Great Exhibition of 1851 he was awarded a medal for the dolls' dresses, although not for the dolls themselves. The jury's verdict on this occasion stated: 'The dolls on which these dresses are displayed present no point worthy of commendation

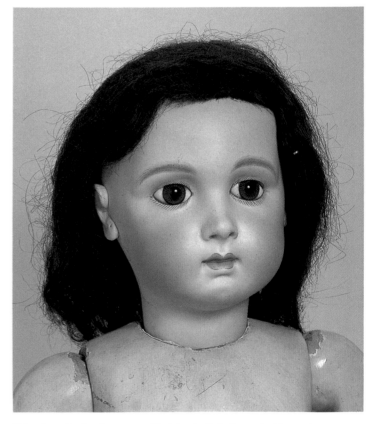

The head of a Jumeau Triste doll **(above),** *French, c. 1875, with composition and jointed wood body, open closed mouth, fixed glass paperweight eyes and a real hair wig.*
33in (84cm)
£10500 ($18585), Sotheby's London 1989

A Jumeau swivel-head pressed bisque character doll **(above far left)**, French, c. 1875, with jointed composition body, fixed blue glass eyes, blonde mohair wig and original cream wool dress.
19¼in (49cm) Sotheby's London 1990

A Jumeau swivel-head bisque doll **(above middle)**, French, c. 1870, with kid body, fixed blue glass paperweight eyes, closed mouth, wig on cork pate and muslin dress.
22in (56cm) Sotheby's London 1990

A François Gaultier bisque doll **(above right)**, French, c. 1880, with jointed wood and composition body, fixed brown glass eyes, closed mouth, real hair wig, dress and bonnet. *16in (41cm) Sotheby's London 1990*

A Jumeau Bébé doll **(left)**, French c. 1890, with wood and composition body, large paperweight eyes, open mouth, holding a Steiff monkey, German, c. 1910.

but the dresses themselves are very beautiful.'

It was not until the 1867 Paris Exposition, where Jumeau won a silver medal, that specific mention is made of dolls' heads. By this time, he had moved to rue d'Anjou-Marais. Around 1862 Emile Jumeau, François' second son, was taking a keen interest in the firm (he claimed to have invented the swivel-head doll, albeit a year too late), and so it must be assumed that the company was heavily involved in producing bisque heads by this date. However, it is not until 1873, when the Jumeaux moved to smart new factory premises at Montreuil-sous-Bois, that they proudly advertised the fact that they were making porcelain dolls' heads.

The new factory was a great step forward for the firm. The traditional method of making dolls, i.e., outworkers constructing the various components in their own homes, often in appalling conditions, finally ended as Jumeau brought together his skilled work-force into one complex. Everyone and everything needed to make the dolls was on site, from the kilns for firing the heads, to the eye-makers, wig-makers, painters, costumiers, and boot-makers—even the boxes in which the dolls were ultimately packed were made on the spot. This amalgamation markedly speeded up manufacture and gave greater quality and quantity control to the management.

The Franco-Prussian war of 1870–71 gave the Jumeau doll factory an even greater impetus, as shrewd Pierre Jumeau used the defeat of the French armed forces as a propaganda and marketing tool. The huge national debt facing France as a result of their defeat by Germany only served to spur national pride further. Artists, industrialists—in fact the whole French nation—strove to rid their land of this shameful debt, which they promptly did, much to German amazement. Anything German-made was despised by the French, and Jumeau was not slow to use this racial hatred as a marketing device. A booklet enclosed with a Jumeau doll as late as the early 1880s ridicules German dolls in no uncertain terms for, among other things, their ridiculous faces, silly eyes, poor bodies, and animal-like cries. In 1873 Jumeau won a gold medal at the Vienna Exhibition, and the French report on the fair stated: 'M. Jumeau of Paris, the first and the most important doll-making house, has freed us from our former obligation to have the foreigner furnish us with porcelain heads.'

The Jumeau firm promoted their dolls all over Europe and the United States, with lavishly dressed

A fine Renou musical automaton of a magician, French, c. 1900, the Jumeau head with blue paperweight eyes. The clockwork and musical mechanisms concealed within the base cause the doll to tap her wand and a grinning head to appear in the magic box.
15½in (39cm) £2750 ($4320), Sotheby's London 1989

dolls posed in equally ornate miniature room settings. They had realized that they could not compete against the Germans for producing low-priced, medium-range dolls, so they concentrated on the top end of the market—hence the fabulous quality of their dolls' bisque heads and the extraordinary luxury of their outfits. Between 1876 and 1878 Pierre resigned, shattered by the premature death of his eldest son to whom the business had been intended to devolve. He handed over the running of the firm to his next son, Emile, whose clever marketing ideas and business acumen served to advance the reputation of the company. In the French Exposition of 1878 Jumeau won yet another gold medal for his dolls. This was perhaps the most well-deserved award of all, as he now had stiff competition from his fellow countrymen Bru, Steiner, Gaultier, and Schmitt, all of whom were well represented in the exhibition. From this time onward the Jumeau bodies were proudly emblazoned with the 'Medaille d'Or' ('Gold Medal') stamp.

By 1882 Jumeau was producing 85,000 dolls a year, and by 1885 he employed five hundred people. He patented numerous designs, among them a voice box operated by a pull-string in 1885 and sleeping paperweight eyes in 1886; in 1888 the first advertisements appeared for open-mouthed Jumeaux with teeth. These innovations helped to increase the demand for his dolls even further, and by 1889 the company claimed to employ one thousand people and to produce 300,000 dolls every year. Jumeau's reign as the king of the dolls was not successfully challenged until the 1885 Paris Exposition, where the house of Bru was also awarded a gold medal, thus obliging the Jumeaux to share the pedestal they had occupied for so long.

The early Jumeau heads, those of the late 1870s and early 1880s, are normally unmarked. They have remarkable bodies whose composition torsos have turned wooden limbs and eight floating ball joints for ease of articulation. The bodies are sometimes stamped with the 'Medaille d'Or' mark in blue. These early dolls are often classified by collectors as 'Portrait Jumeaux' and supposedly they depict actual children, their sculptors having taken their models from life. Whether the designs were derived from living children is open to debate. This could be true, but a more realistic explanation as to the wide variety of heads is that the company was in the early stages of producing bisque heads and so produced a number of different experimental moulds, each with a very short production run, in order to test their varying popularity with the buyers. The dolls were of pressed bisque and the workmanship varied from doll to doll, which again gives the dolls a charm and individuality that the later poured clay dolls do not possess. They tend to have a very white colouring and finely painted eyebrows reminiscent of the Parisiennes that were being produced at the same time. The eyes are extremely large, almond-shaped, and often pale blue.

The second distinct group of Jumeaux are those with the impressed 'E.J.' mark, which is found on the early closed-mouth Bébés. The red 'Tête Jumeau' transfer mark and the 'S.G.D.G.' mark (which means that the doll is sold with a patent, but without a government guarantee, any infringement of this patent leading to litigation by the manufacturer) are found on the dolls of the late 1880s and 1890s. Jumeaux of the 1880s are noted for their wonderfully expressive paperweight eyes, heavily painted and dominant brows, and large painted eyelashes. The eyes are especially remarkable for their size, which is proportionately large in comparison to the rest of the face. Any Jumeau with a closed mouth is preferable to an open-mouthed model, which generally has a less appealing expression, darker face colouring, and is later, its patent being introduced in 1888. Jumeaux with fixed wrists are earlier than those with ball-jointed wrists and, again, are more desirable. The Bébé bodies are quite chunky and well-constructed, consisting of a well-moulded composition torso with wood and composition lower limbs. The blue Jumeau 'Medaille d'Or' stamp normally embellishes the buttocks.

The Long-faced Jumeau, or Jumeau Triste, and the A-mould Jumeaux are the most expensive of all the moulds. These dolls, which were probably produced in the first half of the 1880s, have longer, less-rounded faces, with large applied ears and sad expressions. Whereas the Jumeau Triste is marked on the body and never on the head, the A-mould, which it closely resembles, bears the incised marks 'E.J.A.'. In 1892 Jumeau patented a mulatto or black doll, which appealed to the markets in the French colonies and the Indies; these are relatively scarce and worth looking out for. Another less well-known but desirable rarity is the so-called Phonograph Doll. Thomas Edison's invention of the phonograph was exploited by Jumeau, who advertised his Jumeau Phonograph Doll in time for Christmas 1893. The doll's torso was fitted with a miniature gramophone that played pre-recorded wax cylinders of little girls saying sweet things. They were extremely expensive and the complex mechanism was prone to faults and breaking down, both of which led to the doll—a far-sighted gamble on the part of Emile—being a commercial disaster. Jumeau also produced heads for many of the leading Paris automaton (mechanical doll) manufacturers, another area which Jumeau collectors should consider as an addition to their collections.

THE ULTIMATE FRENCH BEBE, THE BRU

The Bru doll-manufacturing company provided the stiffest competition to Jumeau. Their aim was to produce a doll of superlative quality and beauty and, judging from the dolls that have survived, they certainly succeeded. They were less prolific in their production of dolls than Jumeau and so have the added

Shoulder bisque poupards (above), French, c. 1880. 11in (28cm) and 11½in (29cm) £700 ($1105), Sotheby's London, 1989
A Bru Jeune circle and dot bisque doll and a Bru Jeune bisque doll (opposite above right), French, c. 1875 and 1880.
Both 15¾in (40cm) Sotheby's London 1990
A Bru Jeune black bisque Bébé doll (opposite above far right), French, c. 1875. 12½in (32cm) £9900 ($18415), Sotheby's London 1988
A circle and dot Bru bisque doll (opposite below far right), French, c. 1875. 22in (56cm) £12100 ($22500), Sotheby's London, 1988
A fine, rare circle and dot Bru Jeune pressed bisque Bébé doll (right) French, c. 1875. 29in (74cm) £17600 ($27360) Sotheby's London 1989

cachet today of being rarer and therefore more highly prized and valuable. Many collectors would name the Bru Bébé as the ultimate, most desirable doll to obtain for their collections, as its workmanship and beauty could be said to represent the pinnacle of doll design and manufacture.

Leon Casimir Bru Jeune, the founder of the doll firm Bru Jeune et Cie, is first listed as a manufacturer of dolls with leather bodies in 1868. His factory, like Jumeau's was situated in Montreuil-sous-Bois, with additional workshops in Paris. Although the Parisiennes produced in the late 1860s and 1870s are highly desirable, it is the Bébé, or infant-shaped doll, for which Bru are most famed. The style of the bodies

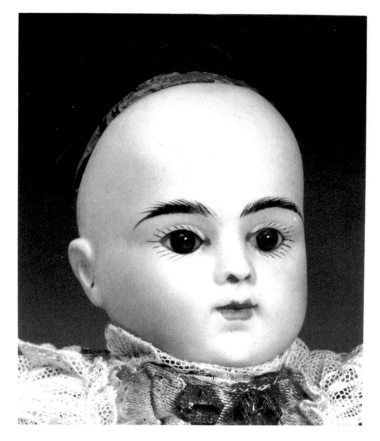

The head of a Bru Jeune bisque doll, French, c. 1875.
Sotheby's London

The head of a Bru Teteur bisque doll, French, c. 1879,
impressed Bru Jne 8 T, with leather body and wooden
arms and legs, open mouth, fixed brown glass eyes and
blonde wig.
18½in (47 cm) £3300 ($6140), Sotheby's London 1989

of the later Bébés bears many resemblances to the Parisienne bodies from which they evolved. They are all swivel-headed dolls, the shoulder plates being moulded with delicate shoulder blades and small breasts, the whole then affixed to jointed bodies covered with kid leather. They are marked in several ways. The early dolls bear the circle and dot or circle and crescent marks on the backs of the necks; the later dolls the impressed 'Bru' or 'Bru Jeune' names. The dolls are often marked both on the backs of the heads and the shoulder plates, with additional paper trade labels pasted across the chest and under the arms. The standard Bru Bébé has wooden lower limbs and finely modelled and tinted bisque lower arms. The faces have soft expressions, enormous paper-weight eyes, and moulded open closed mouths with either moulded teeth or the tip of the tongue showing.

Bru liked to experiment with body types and was one of the first to patent an all-rubber doll. Indeed, innovations and gimmicks were to become a feature of this particular firm, and hardly a year passed without a new patent being brought out for yet another ingenious device. Between 1867 and 1869 Bru obtained patents for Surprise Dolls, which included crying dolls and two-faced dolls. In 1872 yet another was

introduced, this time with a small musical box housed within the torso. Another famous invention of 1879 was the Bébé Teteur, a doll that appeared to suck from a bottle and that remained a popular seller well into the 1890s. By 1885 the company proudly boasted that they had patented twenty-five inventions, including sleeping dolls, eating dolls, kiss-blowing dolls, Oriental and black dolls.

By 1883 the company was run by a Monsieur H. Chevrot, and it is under his leadership and direction that the company achieved the majority of its awards and thereby increased its exports. He in turn handed over management of the firm to Paul Eugène Girard around 1890. Finally, in 1899 the company merged with other French manufacturers to form the Société Française de Fabrication de Bébés et Jouets. Although Bru dolls from c. 1900 onwards were made from the same moulds and were still marked with the Bru name, their quality deteriorated and so these later dolls bear little resemblance to their earlier counterparts. Dolls marked 'Bru Jne R' were probably produced in the very late 1890s or early 1900s. These have crude composition bodies and poor-quality, grainy, highly coloured bisque heads, with none of the delicacy of painting or finish normally associated

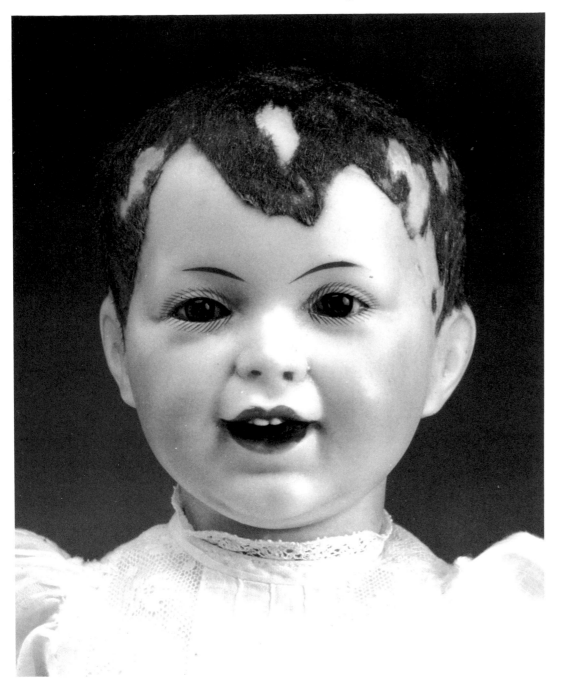

The head of a S.F.B.J. bisque smiling boy character doll, French, c. 1910, impressed 235 6, with moulded open closed mouth and upper teeth, inset blue glass eyes and the remains of an original flocked brown wig. 17¼in (44cm) £825 ($1535), Sotheby's London 1989

with Bru. Although these dolls are still desirable, they are worth a fraction of the cost of a true Bru Jeune. So do not be carried away by the name alone—always take the quality into account before making a purchase.

SOCIETE FRANCAISE DE FABRICATION DE BEBES ET JOUETS

By 1899 the German doll manufacturers were not only successfully competing with the French, they were winning hands down. While the French continued to garner awards at international trade fairs for their fabulous luxury dolls that only the very rich could afford, the Germans produced good-quality dolls priced to suit every pocket. If the French came up with a good idea, the Germans simply adapted it for the mass market. Attitudes to play had also changed. Children demanded dolls that they could

actually handle and actively play with. The expensive French Bébés could only be played with under the strictest supervision; they were not suitable for serious play but for delicate dressing and undressing or simply for looking at and admiring.

As a result of the fierce competition from Germany, the French doll manufacturers realized they would either have to unite or disappear completely. In 1899, they amalgamated to form the Société Française de Fabrication de Bébés et Jouets (S.F.B.J.), which included the majority of the leading manufacturers: Jumeau, Bru, Danel et Cie, Fleischmann & Blödel, Rabery & Delphieu, and others. The dolls produced in the early days of the S.F.B.J. were on the whole crude versions of popular dolls, using the original moulds but made to a much lower standard. A basic dolly-faced model was produced with the mould

Two Armand Marseille My Dream Baby bisque dolls **(above)**, *German, c. 1920. Impressed ÁM 341 (closed mouth) and AM 351 (open mouth).*

An Armand Marseille bisque doll **(left)**, *German, c. 1910, impressed A.M.390, with composition body, brown glass eyes, mohair wig and original gauze clothing. 15½in (39cm) Münchner Stadtmuseum*

A J. D. Kestner bisque character doll **(above, left)**, *c. 1898; a Simon & Halbig bisque doll* **(above, middle)**, *c. 1887; a Hertel Schwab bisque googly doll, c. 1914* **(above, right)**. *16in (41cm), 19in (48cm) and 10in (26cm) Sotheby's London 1990*

numbers of 60 and 301. These have very heavy bisque faces, fixed black or violet eyes, and open mouths with moulded teeth. The fact that these dolls carry Paris markings means that, despite their obvious flaws, they remain popular with modern collectors. They are probably the cheapest French bisque doll that can currently be purchased, albeit at a higher price than a similar low- to medium-quality German doll would generally command.

In 1909 Kämmer & Reinhardt produced the first bisque character doll. It was now the turn of the French to take a German idea and exploit it. The S.F.B.J. character dolls are some of the most interesting dolls ever produced. The quality of their heads is normally good, although the composition and wood

bodies often leave much to be desired. These dolls form the 200 series of character doll mould numbers. Among them are boy dolls, either laughing or crying and with moulded or flocked hair, as well as grinning and pouting babies. They tend to have brilliant inset blue eyes or intaglio eyes that seem very similar to those produced by Heubach. They also produced an interesting number of black dolls for export to their colonies. As the century progressed the decline in standards became more obvious, with celluloid and composition used as cheaper alternatives to bisque.

GERMAN BISQUE DOLLS

Although French dolls reigned supreme in the 1870s and 1880s, by the early 1900s the German doll-makers had taken the lead. They achieved this initially by making good-quality, but cheaper copies of the French bisques, using mass-production methods that led to more widely affordable products within the reach of ordinary families. Secondly, they excelled at making innovative character dolls in the early part of

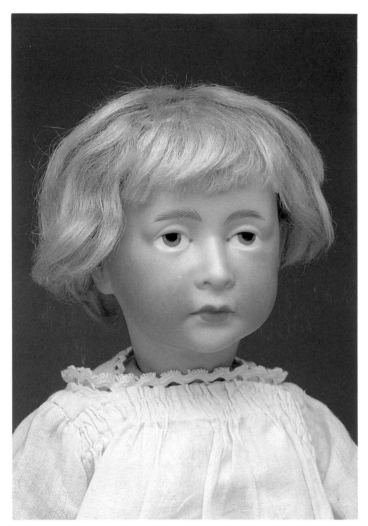

The head of an Armand Marseille bisque character doll, German, c. 1912, impressed A4M, with closed pouting mouth, painted grey-blue eyes, feathered eyebrows. 14in (36cm)
£3850 ($6740), Sotheby's London 1988

A rare Simon & Halbig bisque character doll, German c. 1912, impressed 150 S & H 1, with ball-jointed and wood composition body, fair wig and magician's black robe and hat. 17¾in (45cm)
£10120 ($15890), Sotheby's London 1989

the twentieth century, which the French in turn were forced to copy. Indeed the heads were of such fine quality that many major French doll manufacturers (including Jumeau) imported the German heads to place on their own French-made bodies. Many dolls of this type are just impressed 'DEP', but are fixed onto superior jointed French wood and composition bodies. Leaving off the full manufacturer's marking and country of origin probably made them sell better outside Germany. German bodies of the late nineteenth century tended to be of jointed kid or gusseted fabric, both of which were largely replaced around 1900 by lightweight composition and wood bodies, which were lighter to transport, hence cheaper to sell abroad. By the end of the nineteenth century, the German doll-makers were responsible for producing half the world's total output of dolls. The measure of their success is best reflected by the collapse of the doll-making industry in France and the resultant formation of the S.F.B.J. in 1899, in effect a last-ditch

attempt to compete with Germany.

Sonneberg and other parts of Thüringia had a tradition of doll- and toy-making, rich with both a large, skilled population to provide labour and the basic raw materials required for doll-making. It is no wonder, then, that so many doll-makers and porcelain factories flourished in those regions. The dolls produced in the Walterhausen area of Thüringia were some of the finest, partly as a consequence of the intense rivalry with its neighbour of Sonneberg. Top German doll-makers included Kämmer & Reinhardt, Simon & Halbig, J. D. Kestner, Kley & Hahn, and Alt, Beck & Gottschalck. If we look at just a few of the larger and most prestigious German doll-makers in more detail, the evolution and the success of the German doll industry as a whole can be seen.

ARMAND MARSEILLE

Although not regarded as either the most imaginative or quality-conscious of manufacturers, Armand

An early Simon & Halbig shoulder bisque doll, German, c. 1880, with cloth body and bisque forearms, closed mouth, fixed brown glass eyes and blonde mohair wig. 18in (46cm) £1210 ($2250), Sotheby's London 1988

Shoulder bisque doll, probably Simon & Halbig, German, c. 1865–70, with cloth body, fixed glass spiral eyes and real hair wig. 18³/4in (48cm) £1300 ($2055), Sotheby's London 1989

Marseille can certainly be credited with being the most prolific. His dolls are the most commonly found of all bisque dolls. It has been suggested that the very French-sounding name was actually a marketing device, but recent research has shown that Marseille was indeed of French descent, the Russian-born son of a Huguenot architect. He was an entrepreneur who at the age of twenty-eight bought a porcelain factory in Sonneberg, producing his first bisque head there in 1885. Among the first of the dolls he produced was the 370 mould doll. It is a shoulder-head doll with fixed eyes, mounted on a kid-leather body with composition or bisque lower arms. This was followed by the 1894 mould, which has a bisque head mounted on a composition toddler body and was probably introduced in the year of its mould number. Both of these dolls have more heavily painted brows reminiscent of French dolls. However, the most commonly found bisque doll of all, which must have been produced in staggering quantities, is the 390 mould, which

was introduced around 1915. This is a very pretty doll—at least the first one or two you see are, after that they tend to become a bit boring—on a jointed-wood, toddler body. Between 1924 and 1925 the 'My Dream Baby' was introduced, with the mould number 351 for the open-mouthed baby with two teeth, and 341 for the prettier closed-mouth example, which is slightly more valuable. The dolls were sold wearing simple gauze shifts and shoes, which helped to keep down the production and retailing costs. Because they are readily available and among the least expensive bisque dolls on the market, these are all very good dolls for collectors to start off their collections. Marseille did introduce some more interesting dolls, including Orientals, Red Indians, Googleys, and some very rare character dolls with intaglio eyes. However, even the character dolls, which were produced in relatively small numbers, fail to achieve the same prices as character dolls made by a more highly respected manufacturer such as Kämmer & Reinhardt.

A Kämmer & Reinhardt bisque character doll, German, c. 1911, impressed 116/A 36, with curved limb composition body, open closed mouth and simulated upper teeth, weighted blue eyes and red wig.
14in (36cm) £1760 ($2765), Sotheby's London 1989

An exceptionally rare Kämmer & Reinhardt bisque character doll, German, c. 1910, impressed 105, with six-ball jointed wood and composition body.
21¹/₂in (55cm)
£90200 ($141600), Sotheby's London 1989

Marseille heads are normally well marked with either the full name or the initials. Alternatively, some shoulder-head dolls also bear the horseshoe mark that was also used by Ernst Heubach (joint owner of the Köppelsdorfer Porcelain Works, which produced the dolls' heads).

SIMON & HALBIG

Simon & Halbig was not in the true sense a doll manufacturer, but a manufacturer of dolls' heads, first of porcelain and later celluloid and composition. Their factory was situated in Gräfenhain, Thüringia, and it is believed that they began production in the late 1860s or early 1870s. As little documentary evidence exists, these dates are based on the style of marked early dolls. Simon & Halbig produced heads for a number of manufacturers, the most famous being Kämmer & Reinhardt, Heinrich Handwerck, C. M. Bergmann, and Cuno & Otto Dressel. Although

they made a large quantity of heads, the quality of their output was consistently high. The bisque is of high quality and on the earlier (pre-1890) dolls tends to be extremely white and pale, a reflection of the trends in Paris. The skin tone darkens as the century progresses to a nice healthy pink by 1900.

Presumably Simon & Halbig supplied the heads complete with eyes, as in 1890 they issued two patents for eyes. The first one was for manually moving the lashed eyelids up and down by means of a wire that extended through the back of the doll's head. The second was a similar wire-operated device to move the eyeballs from side to side, thus producing the first flirty-eyed doll (it was not until 1902 that Otto Gans patented the weight-operated flirty eyes with which we are familiar today). The earlier dolls are shoulder-heads, with either painted eyes or, more commonly, fixed paperweight eyes and moulded closed mouths or open closed mouths. They are marked with the

A Kämmer & Reinhardt flirty-eyed baby doll, German,
c. 1920, impressed 126, with composition body and fair
mohair wig.
19in (48cm)
Münchner Stadtmuseum

A Kämmer & Reinhardt Kaiser baby, German, c. 1910,
*impressed K*R, with painted face and hair, original dress*
and richly decorated ornamental cradle in an iron stand.
9½in (24cm)
Münchner Stadtmuseum

initials 'S.H.' and a number either at the back or the front of the shoulder plate. By 1890 the open mouth with inserted teeth was more popular with buyers, the only exception being the character heads, which still continued to have moulded closed mouths. As a general rule any bisque doll with a closed mouth will be more sought after and valuable than an open-mouthed version.

Perhaps the most scarce and desirable of all the character heads produced is the 150 series, with the 151 being slightly more available than the 152, which is probably the rarest of all. Few of these dolls come on the market, and when they do they fetch higher prices than the finest of the French Bébés. The very attractive dolly-faced dolls with the mould numbers 1039, 1078, and 1079 were produced in larger numbers and are still reasonably priced. Lady dolls produced in the early 1900s and Orientals are also very highly prized. The fascinating thing about this

manufacturer is that dolls with previously unlisted mould numbers often come to light, which provides specialist collectors with a great deal of excitement as the collecting boundaries are further enlarged. Simon & Halbig merged with Kämmer & Reinhardt in 1918, a logical progression since the former had produced the majority of their heads for the latter.

When examining a doll's head for marks, take care not to confuse Simon & Halbig's marks—'S & H'—with those of Schoenau & Hoffmeister—'S.★.H.'. The marks are similar, but Schoenau & Hoffmeister's products are inferior and less valuable.

KÄMMER & REINHARDT

Kämmer & Reinhardt's dolls are the most highly collectable of all the German models. They are of a consistently high quality, thanks to the fine bisque of the Simon & Halbig heads, and to the imaginative and ever-changing designs, of which around forty-

Two Kämmer & Reinhardt bisque character dolls (above), German, c. 1910, one impressed 112 34 with open closed mouth, the other impressed 114 39 (Hans) with painted blue eyes and toddler body.
11in (28cm) and 15in (38cm) £4400 ($6910) and £2530 ($3970), Sotheby's London 1989
Two Kämmer & Reinhardt bisque character dolls (left), German, c. 1909, the boy impressed 101 43, the girl impressed 109 39; both with composition and wood bodies.
17in (43cm) and 15½in (39cm) £2310 ($3625) and £4620 ($7255), Sotheby's London 1989

An exceptionally rare bisque character doll, probably by Kämmer & Reinhardt, German, c. 1910, impressed 111, with composition and wood body, closed mouth, painted blue eyes and Steiff dog. 19in (48cm) £11000 ($17270), Sotheby's London 1989

four different head styles are known to exist. At the time of publication the world's most valuable doll is a Kämmer & Reinhardt character impressed 105, which fetched £90,200 ($141,600). This reflects the fierce competition for particularly rare moulds and the lengths that people will go to in order to possess one.

The business was founded in 1885 near Walterhausen by Ernst Kämmer, who was largely responsible for the design and manufacture of the dolls, and Franz Reinhardt, who provided the business know-how. Despite the death of Ernst Kämmer in 1901, the firm continued to trade under the joint names and went from strength to strength. It became even more powerful when it joined forces with the famous Bing brothers of Nuremberg, whose tin-plate toys are widely collected today. This, together with its amalgamation with the Simon & Halbig porcelain factory, made Kämmer & Reinhardt a formidable giant in the doll-making world.

All the dolls were produced with good-quality jointed wood and composition bodies, which have rouged knees and painted finger- and toe-nails. The well-shaped composition limbs were given ease of articulation by means of floating wooden ball joints. Unlike some other manufacturers who were content to produce just the head of reasonable quality, Kämmer & Reinhardt ensured that the entire doll was finished to a very high standard. They were interested in body innovations and produced a number of walking, kiss-blowing, and talking dolls, with primitive voice boxes inserted into the torso and operated by pull-cords.

The most commonly available doll they produced is the 192 mould, which is a very pretty, dolly-faced model. They are normally blue-eyed with long, luxurious blonde wigs. However, Kämmer & Reinhardt's

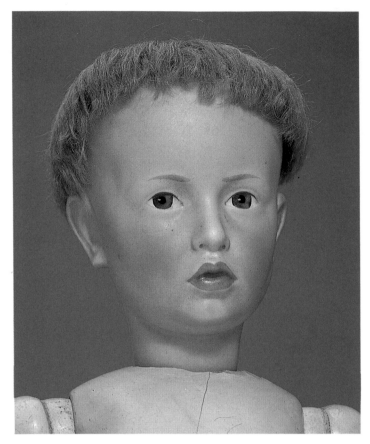

The head of a Kammer & Reinhardt bisque character doll, German, c. 1909, with composition and ball-jointed wood body, painted brown eyes, closed mouth, and blonde wig. Neck chipped at socket. 21¼in (54cm) £13200 ($21120), Sotheby's London, 1990

Two Kämmer & Reinhardt 'Mein Liebling' character dolls, German, c. 1911, one impressed 117 70, the other 117/A 76, one with brown eyes, the other blue. 27½in (70cm) and 30in (76cm) £3300 ($5180) and £3500 ($5495), Sotheby's London 1989

real claim to fame is the invention of the bisque character doll, whose head design was created by a sculptor using an actual child as his model. As a result, many of the character dolls are given names, presumably after the children from whom the designs were taken. The first character doll they produced was in 1909: commonly known as the Kaiser baby, it bears the impressed mark '100'. An ugly little fellow, it has a head with moulded laughing mouth and painted intaglio eyes, mounted onto a curved-limb, six-piece baby body. It was supposedly modelled on the German Emperor's own son, although whether this is true is open to debate. The doll was very successful and encouraged the firm to increase its production. The 101 mould soon followed and is given the names of Peter or Marie, depending on whether it wore a short or long wig. However, the most sought-after mould numbers in this series are as follows: 102, 103, 104, 105, 106, 107 (Carl), 108, 109 (Elise), 111, 112 (Elsa). As already stated, the 105 is the world's most valuable doll—at least for the time being. Character dolls numbered 101, 114 (Hans & Gretchen), 115, 115A, 116, 116A, 117 and 117A (the Mein Lieblings), and 117N, while remaining some of the most expensive of

bisque dolls, are not quite in the same league as the earlier numbers, which are much more difficult to find.

The 117 and 117A, the Mein Liebling bisque doll, is one of the prettiest and most popular dolls, with its rather sad, pensive expression and closed mouth. The two moulds are identical, and so it is hard to understand why the A was incorporated into the numbering of some of the dolls. The 117N has an entirely different face and was produced with both sleeping and flirting eyes. These make about half the price of the Mein Liebling mould. The dolls bearing impressed marks beginning with the number 12 were produced as baby dolls. The 126 mould is an attractive chubby doll with eyes that can flirt roguishly from side to side (incidentally, any interesting eye movement will automatically add value to a doll). The dolls are impressed at the back of the heads with 'K ★ R', 'S & H', the mould number, and the size of the doll in centimetres.

J. D. KESTNER, THE GERMAN JUMEAU
Dolls produced by the Kestner factory are of the highest quality from head to toe. The fine creamy bisque, imaginative designs, and good-quality bodies

Three Kämmer & Reinhardt character dolls (above),
German, c. 1911, all impressed 115/A.
19in (48cm), 13½in (34cm) and 19in (48cm)
£2970 ($4665), £1980 ($3110) and £3740 ($5870),
Sotheby's London 1989

A Rose O'Neill all-bisque Kewpie doll (above), American,
c. 1913.
12¼in (31cm) £880 ($1735), Sotheby's London 1988
A fine, rare J. D. Kestner glass-eyed bisque Kewpie doll
(left), German, c. 1913, impressed O'Neill, JDK 10.
10½in (27cm) £3520 ($6230), Sotheby's London, 1989

were made entirely by Kestner, unlike other manufacturers, who ordered component parts from other
specialist manufacturers. In his desire for excellence
and complete control over the manufacturing process,
J. D. Kestner, Jr, was very similar to Emile Jumeau,
one of his arch-rivals.

Johannes Daniel Kestner was the founding father
of the Walterhausen bisque doll-making industry. He
came from humble stock, the son of a butcher who
supplied the meat for Napoleon's army. It is reputed
that during his travels he became fascinated by the
skills of making papier-mâché and began his own
such business making buttons and small fancy goods
(including dolls). While the buttons and ornaments
were not such a success, the dolls were and so Kestner
concentrated his efforts and skills on these. The business thrived and he later passed it on to his son,
Johannes Daniel Kestner, Jr, who purchased a ceramics factory in Ohrdruf in 1860 and produced bisque

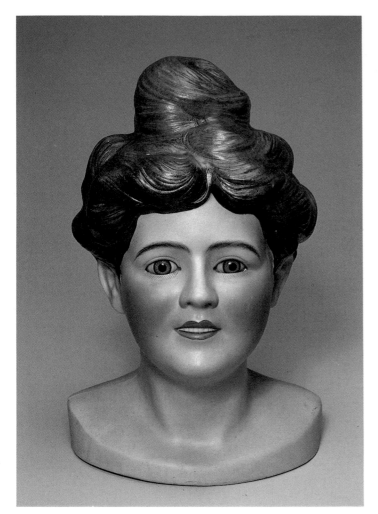

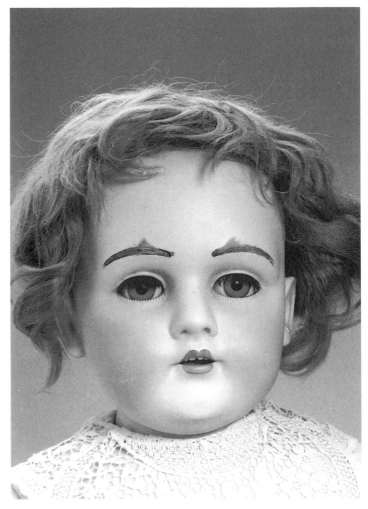

A large bisque Gibson girl head, German, c. 1910, with open closed mouth and moulded teeth, fixed blue glass eyes and moulded hair. 11in (28cm), £1320 ($2110), Sotheby's London 1990

The head of a J. D. Kestner shoulder bisque doll, German, c. 1910, impressed 195, with inserted red hair and mohair eyebrows inserted into the bisque forehead. 29in (74cm) £385 ($715), Sotheby's London 1988

dolls from that date onward. By 1906 he employed a workforce of a thousand.

Although Kestner's dolly-faced, open-mouthed dolls are very desirable, it is the closed-mouth versions, character dolls, Orientals, Googleys, Kewpies, and lady dolls that excite the most interest. The lady doll, or Gibson Girl as she was advertised (after the famous illustrations by Charles Dana Gibson), was introduced in 1910 and epitomized the Edwardian lady in all her elegance and curvaceousness. In 1909 Kestner introduced an interesting but rather peculiar doll that had inserted fur eyebrows. In 1913, by arrangement with the American designer Rose O'Neill, the all-bisque Kewpie doll was produced, its transition from working drawing to bisque figure supervised in the German factory by O'Neill herself.

Although many of Kestner's fine dolls bear the incised 'J. D. K.' mark, some have only mould numbers. It is strange that such fine dolls should be left without any easily identifiable markings. If there is any doubt

that your doll is truly a Kestner, check its pate. If it is made of a plaster-like substance, it is almost certainly by him. Some extremely beautiful but unmarked shoulder-head dolls made in the 1860–70 period sometimes come on the market. These are very reminiscent in their design of poured wax dolls produced in England at that date, with their heads turned slightly to one side. They bear the famous plaster pates and so have been attributed to Kestner. In my opinion, of all the German dolls produced, these are unrivalled for their sheer excellence of manufacture and design.

GEBRÜDER HEUBACH

Gebrüder Heubach (the Heubach Brothers) was another long-established German firm. Little is known about the individual men, only that the company was originally founded in 1820. By 1863 the successors of Gebrüder Heubach made bisque dolls' heads in Lichte near Wallendorf, Thüringia, while the dolls' bodies were probably produced and assembled in Sonneberg,

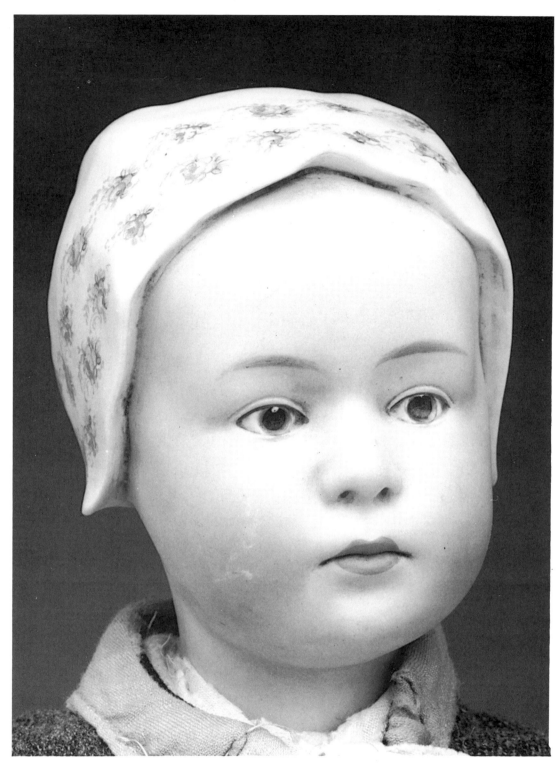

8192
Germany
Gebrüder Heubach

HEU
BACH

G   H

One of the more common marks found on Gebrüder Heubach dolls (above). A Gebrüder Heubach baby Stuart bisque character doll (left), German, c. 1912, impressed 7977, with jointed wood and composition body. 17in (43cm) £715 ($1330), Sotheby's London 1988

A Gebrüder Heubach whistling boy bisque doll (below), German, c. 1914, impressed 1774, with cloth body. 14¹/₂in (37cm) £385 ($605), Sotheby's London 1989

which was the firm's official trading address. They produced a huge quantity of porcelain ware, not only dolls' heads but a wide variety of ornaments to adorn the Edwardian mantelpiece. Some ornaments are in the form of large crying or smiling babies, while others are courting or bicycling couples (the latter complete with miniature metal bicycles). There are even smaller baby figurines, which are now called piano babies and comprise an interesting collecting field in their own right. However, the company is best known for its character children, the majority with painted intaglio eyes and lively or sad expressions. Gebrüder Heubach

produced a number of dolls with moulded hair and ribbons, or even bonnets, as in the case of the Baby Stuart doll. Although the dolls' heads are interesting and of good quality, less attention was paid to the bodies, which are often rather crude. The dolls are impressed at the shoulder plates and backs of the heads with either the name 'Heubach' in a square logo or a stylized sunburst. The mould numbers normally comprise four figures that start with the numbers 5, 6 or 7. This company should not be confused with that of Ernst Heubach, who also produced dolls, but of an inferior quality.

FABRIC DOLLS

ALTHOUGH SOME FINE AMERICAN NINETEENTH-CENTURY DOLLS DO SURVIVE, THE HEYDAY OF THE COLLECTABLE FABRIC DOLL WAS THE 1910s TO 1930s, WITH SOME OF THE FINEST EXAMPLES BEING PRODUCED IN GERMANY, ITALY AND ENGLAND.

Fabric dolls have existed for centuries as inexpensive home made playthings for children. Few early examples have survived, for one reason because they were humble items (and thus not worth keeping as heirlooms) and also because of the inherent fragile nature of textiles. A small number of ancient examples are extant, however, including some discovered with mummified remains in Egyptian tombs; there are also Greek and Roman rag dolls preserved in various museums. Primitive civilizations or settlers with no ready access to commercially made toys made their own dolls from whatever scraps of fabric or animal hide were available. However, it is not until the nineteenth century that fabric dolls were produced on a commercial basis and lost their label of being the poor child's toy.

The name Steiff is probably best associated with the production of stuffed teddy bears, toys that the German company claims to have invented. However, the felt character dolls and toys produced by Steiff from 1894 to the 1930s deserve wider general acclaim. They are not only superbly made but also imbued with a great sense of humour and charm. It was in Giengen, Wurttemberg, in 1894 that Margarete Steiff

advertised her factory as the first to make fabric toys. We know that the Montanaris exhibited rag dolls on their stand at the 1851 Great Exhibition in London. However, it is Steiff's mass-production methods based under one roof that are most significant. In the nineteenth century the vast majority of dolls were still produced by outworkers who were paid by the number of items they completed. By 1908 Steiff employed two thousand workers, even then maintaining, as she had in the past, that she personally checked every toy made there. She had begun by making fabric dolls from scraps of unwanted felt supplied by a nearby factory. Her dolls are characterized by a central seam that runs down the faces and by black shoe-button eyes. The figures have applied felt ears that bear the famous 'Knopf im Ohr' (Button in Ear), which she registered in Germany as her trademark in 1905. Sometimes the

*A good Käthe Kruse Du Mein fabric doll (**above left**), German, c. 1927, with cloth body, painted face and hair, and original Irish costume.*
19in (48cm)
£2200 ($3455), Sotheby's London 1989

buttons were removed from the ears of the dolls by zealous parents who were afraid their children might swallow them. Even if the stud has been removed there should be a small puncture hole in the ear where it once was. On the very early toys and dolls a small, plain pewter button will be found, or that bearing the logo of a small elephant. From around 1905 onwards the name of Steiff is clearly visible on the button.

Steiff toys and dolls can easily provide enough interest and variety for collectors to concentrate exclusively on them. Hundreds of different character dolls, toys, and bears were made. I particularly like them because they often poke fun at establishment figures, for example, army officers, policemen, even smug-looking students from Heidelberg University. Fat old men, dwarfs with red noses, clowns, mischievous-looking children, and ethnic characters—among them an Irish footman, a Chinaman, a Polish workman, and a rotund German resplendent in lederhosen—were all subjects employed with great success by Steiff. These toys probably appealed as much to the parents buying them as to the children for whom they were intended. The figures vary in size from about 7–18in (18–46cm). The character dolls have enormous out-

Three fine, rare Steiff Dachau peasant musicians, German, c. 1911, each bearing one or two Steiff studs to the ears, with original felt outfits and musical instruments. 12¼in (31cm)
£4800 ($8400), Sotheby's London 1988

sized feet, which not only add to their visual amusement but actually enable them to stand up. When Margarete Steiff died in 1909 the company was taken over by her nephews. Today Steiff products continue to be made, the humorous, well-made, appealing toys still delighting children, just as they have in the past. The Giengen factory boasts a small museum where collectors can seek advice on their own Steiff pieces or simply visit and admire the fine collection.

The other most famous German producer of fabric dolls was Käthe Kruse. She began her great doll empire quite humbly—by designing and making dolls for her own children. As a mother she was in a good position to judge what would appeal to youngsters, and also, importantly, to parents. To interest children, dolls have to be fully movable, look realistic, and be fun to play with; to interest parents they have to be tough,

A Chad Valley Princess Elizabeth fabric doll, English, c. 1930, with velvet body, felt face and glass eyes, mohair wig, original tiered velvet dress but lacking hat and coat. 17½in (44.5cm) £180, Christie's London 1988

durable, washable, unbreakable, and incapable of harming the child. Kruse's first doll was made in 1907 from a humble domestic towel. She spent the following three years perfecting the design and finish of the doll before trying to market it on a commercial basis. Max Kruse, her husband, was a well-known Berlin sculptor and no doubt he helped her to design the all-important doll's head. Kruse chose as her model a seventeenth-century Italian sculpture, of a head by François Duquesnoy (1597–1643), known as Il Fiam-

mingo. For several years she collaborated with well-known established doll-makers, first with Kämmer & Reinhardt and secondly with Fischer, Naumann & Co of Ilmenau, Thüringia. Neither joint venture was successful—Mrs Kruse was unsatisfied with the quality of dolls both firms produced—so around 1910 she took the bold step of opening her own doll-works.

Kruse's dolls are essentially stitched shells of calico with waterproof seams, and their hand-painted faces are highly detailed and expressive. They are stamped

Two Käthe Kruse rag dolls, German, c. 1918 and 1930.

Two Käthe Kruse dolls, German, c. 1928, with linen-covered bodies, real blonde hair and painted faces. The extra clothes and accessories belong to the boy doll. 19in (49cm) and 19½in (50cm) £500 ($785) and £800 ($1255), Sotheby's London 1989

with the Kruse name in purple ink on the sole of the left foot. In 1911 an issue of *Playthings* magazine described the production methods of Kruse dolls:

> The muslin for the head having been correctly cut out, the reverse side is chemically treated. It is then sewed together and the empty space filled with wadding. In the same way, but without the use of chemicals, the lifelike body is made. Mrs Kruse copies the head from a bambino of the Renaissance period, and her own children are models for the bodies. Here mother-love guides the hand. The muslin is good for painting—the features are painted in. Then they are sprayed with fixative, and the doll is washable.

One of the most desirable Kruse dolls for modern collectors is the 'Schenkerle', or Sand Baby. Filling the doll's body with sand gave it the realistic weight and the floppy feel of a newborn baby. They were so realistic that many of these dolls were purchased by maternity hospitals in order to help their staffs teach young mothers the necessary nursery skills. Perhaps the most desirable of all the Kruse rag dolls is the 'Schlenkerchen' or Laughing Baby and would certainly be regarded as the gem of any Kruse collection. This is closely followed by the 'Du Mein', a baby doll with a sad expression and downturned mouth. Perhaps the rarest, if not the most desirable is the Bambino, a tiny doll of up to 9in (23cm) in height which was intended to be the doll's own doll.

As the Kruse dolls were all made by hand they were expensive and today remain one of the most expensive forms of collectable fabric doll.

A Norah Wellings sailor doll, English, c. 1935.

FABRIC DOLLS

A collection of Lenci rag dolls, Italian, 1930s, from left to right comprising a mascotte doll, a golfer, a Fascist boy, a typical pressed felt doll and a costume doll.
9in (23cm), 16½in (42cm), 13½in (34cm), 10in (25.5cm) and 9½in (24cm)
£100 ($157), £990 ($1555), £638 ($1000), £308 ($485) and £352 ($550), Sotheby's London 1989

*Two Lenci cloth dolls (**below**), Italian, c. 1922, with bodies seamed and jointed at necks, shoulders and hips, pressed felt faces and brown eyes.*
18in (46cm) and 12½in (32cm)
£800 ($1415), Sotheby's London 1989

*A Lenci pressed felt doll (**below**), Italian, c. 1935, with swivel-jointed body, painted face and brown eyes.*
13in (33cm)
£240 ($380), Sotheby's London 1989

*A Lenci cloth doll (**above**), Italian, c. 1930, with stiffened body swivel-jointed at the hips and shoulders and a pressed felt swivel head with painted face.*
16½in (42cm)
£400 ($710), Sotheby's London 1989

In the 1920s a new doll concept was introduced by the doll-makers and embraced by the general public: the 'Art Doll'. This was a doll intended to appeal not only as a plaything for children but as a fashion accessory for young women. The doll-makers commissioned artists and sculptors to design the heads and they were marketed as bona fide works of art.

Perhaps the greatest exponent of the Art Doll was the Italian company Lenci, which produced superb felt dolls with colourful, well-designed outfits and appealing faces. Their producer claimed they were popular with children ranging in age from 5 to 10 and they further asserted that 'Every Lenci Doll is made in Italy by Italian Artists and is an Individual Work of Art'. The Turin company was owned by Enrico Scavini, who named it Lenci after the pet name of his wife, Elena. Lenci dolls are of extremely high quality with pressed felt faces. They are normally in the form of young children with a variety of countenances, all defined by their eyes. There are painted eyes glancing coyly to one side; round, startled orbs with long painted lashes; surprised expressions; or sad, mournful looks. The costumes are of stylish, brightly coloured felt, often in harlequin, chequerboard, or floral patterns. Lenci produced a sporting series, whose felt figures came complete with tennis rackets or golf bags. The most desirable Lenci doll is the felt, svelte

Rudolph Valentino, dressed in his film role as 'The Sheik', which first appeared in the 1927–28 catalogue and was obviously intended for the avid female film-goer.

Unfortunately Lenci dolls are not always marked with their maker's name. On some of the dolls produced in the 1920s and '30s, the name Lenci in flowing script will be stamped onto a foot. Others, if still in their original costumes, will have a pewter button stamped with the Lenci name attached to the chemise. The majority simply had a cardboard tag bearing the Lenci name, which was soon removed and lost. Collectors should beware, however, as there were numerous cheap copies made of the expensive Lenci dolls. It is particularly hard to differentiate between the genuine Lencis and the copies, because in some cases they are almost identical (especially as the quality of post-Depression Lenci dolls declined). Quality therefore cannot be the sole determining factor when trying to decide if a doll is a Lenci or a fake. The only sensible way of telling the differences between the two is by consulting Lenci catalogues (which have been reprinted and are generally available today) and by comparing the construction of the bodies. Lenci dolls tend to have pink felt bodies with the tops of the jointed legs cutting high up into the thigh.

In the 1920s Britain became a major producer of

Two Lenci cloth dolls (below), Italian, 1930s, both with painted faces, brown eyes and blonde mohair wigs. Both 16in (41cm) £1210 ($2250), Sotheby's London 1988

Two Norah Wellings cloth dolls (left), English, 1925–1930, with seamed bodies, swivel jointed at necks, shoulders and hips, pressed felt faces, and painted features. 15in (38cm) and 30¼in (77cm) Sotheby's London 1989

Two Steiff felt dolls (right), German, c. 1908. 10¼in (26cm) and 14½in (37cm) £935 ($1740), Sotheby's London 1988

fabric dolls. The Chad Valley company began in 1823 as a printing and bookbinding business belonging to Anthony Bunn Johnson. The firm was originally based in Birmingham but in 1897 the factory was moved to the village of Harbourne near Birmingham, next to the River Chad. In 1919 the company registered the trade name of Chad Valley. By now under the direction of Johnson's sons and grandsons, Chad Valley specialized in felt and velvet dolls and figures taken from cartoon strips and films, for example, Bonzo Dog (1920), Mabel Lucie Attwell dolls (1920s) and Snow White and the Seven Dwarfs (1938), together with boudoir dolls and teddy bears. As always, the royal family proved a good commercial subject and dolls of the young princesses Elizabeth and Margaret Rose, complete with felt outfits of pale pink, blue, or yellow—the Queen Mother's favourite colours—were made between 1930 and 1938. These attractive dolls had curly mohair wigs, felt faces, inset glass eyes (an advance patented by Chad Valley in 1925), and the hygienically stuffed bodies found on all Chad Valley toys. They were sold at the express wish of the Duke and Duchess of York for the sum of one guinea, as they did not wish the doll to be out of reach of families of average means. Chad Valley dolls are normally marked on the soles of the feet by means of fabric labels.

Norah Wellings (*fl.*1919–59) started her doll-designing career with Chad Valley. She worked with them for seven years before setting up her own company, the Victoria Toy Works, in Wellington, Shropshire. Her brother Leonard handled the administrative, commercial side of the business, while Norah concentrated on designing the dolls and overseeing their production. On 24 November, 1926, she obtained a patent for a fabric or felt head, backed with buckram and lined on the inner surface with a coating of plastic. The head was finished with a waterproof coating that was supposed to make the doll suitable for washing. All of Norah Wellings' creations possess impish, mischievous faces. They either have painted or inserted glass eyes, but the majority have very pronounced, separately applied stick-out ears. Most of the large Atlantic ocean liners carried Norah Wellings sailor dolls, with the name of that particular ship on their cap bands; these were sold as mascots on board the vessels—and proved ideal souvenirs for children. These are among the more common Norah Wellings dolls to be found and are therefore relatively inexpensive to buy now. She produced a large number of fabric dolls depicting children from different lands, including a Maori boy, South Sea Islander, Cowboy, Mountie, and Chinese girl. They vary in size from about 8–30in (20–75cm). Her dolls bear printed fabric labels either

*A Chad Valley Bambina cloth doll (**above left**), English, c. 1936, with velvet-covered body jointed at shoulders and hips.*
17¼in (44cm) £450 ($795), Sotheby's London, 1989
*A Steiff clown doll (**above right**), German, c. 1913, with stitched felt body, swivel head and limbs.*
17in (43cm) £1265 ($1985), Sotheby's London 1989
*Boudoir doll (**right**), French, late 1920s.*

at the wrist or, more commonly, on the soles of the feet.

Dean's Rag Book Co. Ltd was founded in 1905 and specialized in printing colourful books made of fabric. It was a subsidiary of Dean & Son, the London printing and publishing company established in the eighteenth century. Dean's rag books were fully washable and were suitable, so the line went, for children 'who wear their food and eat their clothes'. The books became doll-shaped around 1908, and progressed to become printed calico sheets which, when cut out and sewn together, formed rag dolls. These have evolved into the commercially produced, ready-made dolls with which today's collectors are more familiar. In the 1920s Dean's employed the American designer Grace Wiederseim to produce a series of printed fabric dolls with round 'goo-goo' eyes and piglike snoutish noses. Artists and illustrators such as Cecil Aldin, Hilda Cowham and John Hassall also designed dolls for Dean's. Famous cartoon figures such as Minnie and Mickey Mouse (1930s), Dismal Desmond (1923) and Popeye (1938) were made of printed velvet. The Disney pieces in particular are very popular today, as indeed is any piece of Disneyana dating from the 1930s.

Fabric portrait dolls of King Edward VIII produced by J. K. Farnell and Co. are also worthy of mention.

The dolls had to be withdrawn from sale upon the king's abdication and are consequently highly prized rarities. The young monarch comes dressed in military uniform or Highland dress.

Fabric dolls have long proved popular toys in the United States, where the need for hard-wearing, inexpensive toys suitable for the rugged frontier life was recognized far earlier than in Europe. Two of the best-known fabric doll-makers were Rhode Island-based Izannah Walker and Martha Chase. Although Izannah Walker of Central Falls registered her first patent for stockinette rag dolls in 1873, some of these rare and beautiful dolls date from the mid-1850s, as the hairstyles and original costumes testify. She made her dolls by pressing together glue-coated layers of inexpensive cloth in moulds to form the head and facial features. When they had dried and solidified a soft padding layer was added, followed by a layer of stockinette. They were again stitched or glued to the existing shell and placed once more in the press. The shoulder-heads were then attached to the gusseted fabric bodies and the hair and facial features painted in so as to imitate the expensive German dolls of the same date, with soft black curls framing the faces.

The dolls made by Martha Chase of Pawtucket were constructed in a similar but somewhat more simplified manner than the Walker dolls, a layer of stockinette

A Dean's Rag Book Company velvet rabbit, 'Oswald',
English, c. 1927, with swivel head, printed features and
blue and white cotton slippers.
19³⁄₄in (50cm)
£500 ($785), Sotheby's London, 1989

A large Dean's 'Princess' girl doll, English, c. 1925.

being stretched over a mask with raised features, glued and painted in oils. Impasto was then painted onto the head to give a rougher, more hairlike texture. Martha Chase is reputed to have owned an Izannah Walker rag doll as a child, which was the inspiration for the designs of her own later dolls. By 1910 the dolls were being mass-produced and by 1922 nineteen different models were in production. The Chase dolls have separately applied ears and thumbs, crudely painted faces, and are marked either on the thigh or under the arm, although these have often been rubbed off. The dolls are very popular in North America.

One of the most affordable types of fabric doll to be found today is the Boudoir doll. These were produced in large quantities by unknown French makers. The dolls were intended (like some of those by Lenci) for adult women rather than for child's play. As early as 1910 the great Parisian couturier Paul Poiret was advocating that women carry dolls as fashion accessories. Boudoir dolls were therefore designed to appeal to the young woman rather than the child. They have very sophisticated painted mask faces with dark shaded eyelids, loosely applied skeins of looped silk for hair (often ash blonde à la Jean Harlow), and elongated bodies with plaster lower arms and legs (the latter terminating in tiny gilded high-heeled shoes). They were intended to adorn a woman's boudoir as a piece

of decorative female frippery. Both Dean's Rag Book and Chad Valley produced versions.

Today the most desirable, expensive, and highly collected of the widely available fabric dolls are those made by Käthe Kruse and Margarete Steiff, closely followed by the Italian firm of Lenci. Prices for early American dolls vary as they are harder to find and condition varies enormously from piece to piece. Although an Izannah Walker would be a pleasure and a crowning glory for any doll collector to possess, they are now extremely rare and seldom available outside the United States.

On the other hand, British fabric dolls are inexpensive and probably a good present-day investment. On the whole these examples tend to fetch less at present than bisque dolls from the same period. Unmarked dolls or those by unidentified manufacturers are inexpensive in comparison to the Chad Valley or Norah Wellings-type dolls. At the lower end of the market are the French Boudoir dolls, which were cheaply mass-produced in the 1920s and 1930s. However, when purchasing one of these dolls always make sure that the costume is totally original. 'Boudoirs' were marketed at the time as 'Fashion dolls', and if their costumes are altered, incomplete, or missing you should seriously consider whether the item is worthy of becoming a part of your collection.

CELLULOID (PYROXYLIN) DOLLS

ONE OF THE MOST UNDERPRICED

AND UNAPPRECIATED AREAS OF DOLL

COLLECTING, THEY PROVIDE AN

INTERESTING AND INEXPENSIVE

FIELD FOR THE NEW COLLECTOR.

Celluloid is one of the earliest forms of man-made plastic and was originally invented in the mid-nineteenth century. It was first of all used to simulate ivory, tortoiseshell and horn in the form of haircombs, fans and other fancy goods; but not used for producing dolls until 1869 when the Hyatt brothers of New York used it under the tradename of the Celluloid Novelty Company.

Celluloid is a mixture of cellulose nitrate, camphor pigments, fillers and alcohol. The doll head is produced by placing sheets of celluloid into two moulds which form the front and the back sections. Hot air or steam is then piped into the mould chambers which forces the celluloid to the shape of the mould. The two pieces are then joined together by ether. If a dull finish is required on the head then it is sanded with pummice or a similar scouring compound to remove the shine.

Doll manufacturers were always on the lookout for an unbreakable, durable and lightweight alternative to bisque. As export tariffs were prohibitive and were calculated according to the weight of the goods, they were anxious to find an attractive alternative that was lighter than bisque and therefore cheaper to export: J. D. Kestner, Kämmer & Reinhardt, Bruno Schmidt, Käthe Kruse, Konig & Wernicke, S.F.B.J. all marketed dolls with celluloid heads. Major specialist manufacturers of celluloid who supplied heads to the main doll-makers and who also marketed dolls under their own tradenames are listed as follows:

Germany:Rheinische Gummi and Celluloid Fabrik Co. (probably the most famous of all, whose wares are marked with a turtle logo); Buschow & Beck, Minerva trademark (helmet symbol); E. Maar & Sohn, Emasco trademark (3M symbol);

France: Peticolin (eagle symbol); Société Nobel Française (dragon symbol); Société Industrielle de Celluloid (Sicoine);

United States: Parsons-Jackson Co.

The majority of celluloids produced in the late nineteenth and early twentieth centuries were mounted onto fabric bodies with celluloid lower limbs. The disadvantages of the early celluloids are that they were

A celluloid doll with moulded hair, c. 1930

highly flammable, squashable, subject to fading in light and many bore very hard, shiny complexions that proved unpopular with children.

Although the celluloids produced before 1900 were expensive items, they are now sadly regarded as the poor relation of the bisque versions which they imitate and consequently are still relatively inexpensive for the modern collector. If a rare Kämmer & Reinhardt character doll is too expensive for your budget, think about buying a celluloid copy instead. Hollow, lightweight all-celluloid dolls made in Japan in the 1920s and '30s with painted or inset celluloid eyes and moulded, tinted hair are among the least expensive of the celluloids.

MAINTENANCE AND CONSERVATION

The best advice I could give to any new collector is 'Do as little as possible to your dolls'. I once visited a doll museum and was horrified to see that practically every single doll had been dressed in the most awful frou-frou way and, furthermore, that the owners proudly boasted of the fact! Before bringing in a doll for valuation, many clients used to throw out the doll's old clothes and make nice new nylon lace numbers specially for the occasion. They were then dismayed to learn that they had reduced the value of their doll. To this end, it is important to keep dolls in as original a condition as possible. Only if the doll is seriously damaged or completely nude should radical repairs or re-dressing be considered.

Obviously, if a doll's head is severely damaged, so much so that the visual appearance of the piece is badly impaired, then restoration should be considered. However, I would strongly advise that you inspect other, similar items that the restorer has completed before actually commissioning him or her to start work on your own doll. Some dolls look better damaged than after the restorer has finished with them, so proceed with caution. Particularly unpleasant is the high coloured finish that is often used to disguise a crack or repaired surface. Good restorers are expensive, but their equipment, experience and expert knowledge

usually justify their costs. Repairs to a doll's head by a top restorer, for instance, may only be visible under ultraviolet light and not to the human eye. If damage to the head is your problem, you may in fact find that a visit to a qualified, experienced local ceramic restorer is preferable to a trip to a doll hospital. Good restoration is an expensive process, however, so it is probably a worthwhile undertaking only if you own a particularly rare and valuable piece, or if the doll is of such great sentimental value that financial considerations become secondary. If the doll is one commonly found you might be able to purchase an identical replacement head for less than the cost of restoration. Remember, too, that the value of a restored doll will never be the same as that of a perfect example. All these above mentioned points must be carefully considered before embarking on any course of action. Some minor damage does not need the services of a professional, for example hairline cracks. These can be dealt with inexpensively at home by inserting a tiny spot of glue at each terminating point. Of course, it will not make the crack go away, but it should halt its progress and prevent it from getting worse.

Firing cracks are different to hairlines, the latter resulting from the head being dealt a blow. Firing cracks occur due to separation of clay during the actual firing process (they often appear along the top rim of a bisque head, where the stress is greatest on the clay). Such cracks are not regarded with quite the same horror as hairlines, but collectors should make a mental note of them on their dolls. Always handle those particular pieces with enormous care, since bad handling can lead to hairlines issuing from the firing crack. Again, a tiny drop of glue at the base of the crack should help prevent this from happening. Sometimes the clay will separate slightly along the mould lines at the side of the bisque head, but these should be regarded as firing flaws and not as major defects.

Although the heads of bisque dolls can safely be washed, as all the head colouring has been fixed by firing, their bodies should be left well alone. Those of the painted composition variety, for example, are protected by a very thin coating of water-based varnish which, once removed, is irreplaceable, leaving the body with a horrible bleached, matt surface. Dolls given baths by their little owners often suffer in this way. Similarly, you should avoid washing any composition heads. Areas of painted wood on the bodies, such as lower arms and hands, can be washed gently with liquid soap and a little water. However, if these areas already show signs of deterioration it is best to leave them well alone. There is no effective cleaner for kid-leather bodies, so these too should not be tampered with. Dolls with fabric bodies are usually joined together at the shoulder plate, so you should determine whether you are going to be able to satisfactorily refix this to the body if you take it apart. If you decide you can do this safely—and the body really is disgustingly dirty—then carefully hand-wash it in a pure soap solution. Never use biological detergents, and wash the bodies only in the most dire circumstances.

Bisque and parian heads can be washed using cotton wool and swabs, liquid soap and a little water; wipe the soap and water away with a damp cloth. Never use toothbrushes or nailbrushes on dolls' faces, as some older books have advised. This scouring action damages the surface of the face and can actually remove some of the colour, which in turn leads to devaluation. When cleaning the dolls be extra careful around the eye areas, as you may end up soaking off or damaging the applied real-hair eyelashes and allowing water into the inside of the head.

Glazed china heads are just as simple to clean as any glazed item of domestic porcelain. Simply use a damp cloth and soap solution and wipe clean.

The cleaning and repair of wax and wax-over-composition dolls presents more problems. There are few experienced restorers in this field and they are far-flung. Repair should only be undertaken by an expert—do not attempt to repair damage of any kind yourself. A local museum may be able to recommend a nearby specialist, and the major auction houses usually have lists of restorers. The auctioneers may not have seen the work of all of the individual people they hold on their files, but the names are probably a good starting-off point. It is then up to the collector to inspect examples of their work and to compare their prices.

Do not attempt to clean wooden dolls. Their painted, gessoed heads are protected by a thin coating of varnish, which is their only protection against the outside elements. Dust if you must, but that is all!

Wax, waxed composition and wooden dolls are all affected by humidity and temperature changes. It is for this reason that the seventeenth-century wooden dolls in museums are frequently stored and displayed in a purpose-built temperature- and humidity-controlled chamber. Unfortunately such measures are beyond the means of most collectors, so sensible storage and display are the best preventive measures at your disposal. Never keep these dolls in a centrally heated room and never store them in any place where they are subject to great fluctuations in temperature. In fact, try to move them as little as possible. Never set them in display cabinets with internal overhead lighting, nor in direct sunlight. I have yet to see a satisfactory repair to an early wooden doll, even when undertaken by experts, so there is no doubt that prevention in this case is definitely preferable to any cure.

The problem with collecting fabric dolls is that they can rarely be cleaned effectively. You should avoid washing dolls with felt or fabric faces – even those dolls originally produced as 'washable', since any waterproofing probably wore away years ago, and you simply cannot be sure of its reliability. Nothing much can be done to repair moth damage to the face either. Moth damage to the bodies is more easily remedied, however. Leaky stuffing can be dealt with by simple patching using similar fabrics—and great care.

Most bisque dolls will at some point need restringing. This is a simple and satisfying operation to undertake. If you have not learned this skill, there are specialist restoration books that explain the process in detail. Perhaps the best way to learn is from a fellow doll collector who can guide you through the various stages step by step. Doll societies not only provide a forum for discussing new research and comparing prices, but they also offer fellowship, advice and often cut-price repair materials. If you do not feel confident to carry out restringing on your own, any reputable doll hospital should be able to do this for you quickly and efficiently. In restringing a doll it is important that it not be done too tightly, as this will cause the head to press down into the neck socket and hence do damage. Likewise, take care that it is not too slack, or else the head will loll about in a dangerous fashion.

Too-tight stringing is the most common fault, causing erosion to the neck, hip and arm sockets as the limbs and head are forced in on the body, so pay particular note of this, either when restringing on your own or having it done by an expert. If you are unhappy with any professional restoration job, do not be afraid to insist that it be done again properly. No restoration of any kind should cause further damage or make the doll look worse than it did before the work was undertaken.

Modern doll collectors have a distinct advantage over earlier enthusiasts:

- replacement eyes, hands, teeth, wigs, limbs are widely available
- bodies are now reproduced and sold extensively
- specialist firms offer their products through magazines
- doll fairs both local and international provide an effective network of contacts for the exchange of information.

These replacement items are never quite the same as the originals, but if this is all that is available to you and the appearance of the doll is improved, then why not? Purists sometimes feel that they would rather stick to genuine, original pieces—and so they purchase damaged dolls and duly cannibalize them—but this is a more expensive and time-consuming exercise (though with rewarding results).

COSTUMES

The costume a doll wears makes an enormous visual impact. It is always a joy to come across a doll that is wearing the original clothes made for it, so great care should be taken to conserve such an outfit.

Cotton

In the first half of the nineteenth century, dolls were normally dressed in inexpensive printed cottons, with the original owner acting as seamstress. Take the following precautions with costumes:

- if you intend to wash any printed cotton, test a small area first to see if the dyes are colourfast
- hand-wash the costumes using pure soap flakes only
- never wash a fragile cotton dress because it will only be further damaged: you do not want to end up with a handful of rags rather than the dress you started off with
- pay particular attention to any cotton garments of the late eighteenth and early nineteenth centuries with brown and black dyes printed on them. These colours corrode and corrupt the cotton ground over the years and even leave holes in the cloth.

Silk

Any costume made from silk (as were many French examples in the late nineteenth century) should be examined by a specialist textile conservator, whose expert advice you should take. Many of the late nineteenth-century silks were treated with washes of tin which helped to give the fabric its luxurious weight and sheen. Unfortunately this also ate into the fabric little by little, causing many taffeta garments and trimmings to become brittle and crack—leaving you ultimately with little mounds of dust. This damage is irreversible and irreparable. Therefore

- do not attempt to clean any silk garment yourself
- keep a photographic record of the doll in the deteriorating gown, particularly if the decay is caused by the tin wash on the silk. There is nothing you can do about this.

COSTUME REPLACEMENT

If a doll's costume is well past conserving, only then should you think of replacing it with a near identical copy. Before removing the costume

- photograph the doll front and back
- then carefully peel off the original garments
- take care to keep the original garments carefully as they will provide the basis for creating the new costumes
- take the pattern, if you can, from the old costume and use it for the new one
- match the fabric of the old as closely as possible
- store the original costume, wrapped in acid-free tissue, in a damp, moth-free environment.

If a doll has no dress at all, or you think it has been re-dressed by someone at a later date, then you should consult reference books on fashion, visit museums, or inspect friends' collections to see if you can locate a doll of a similar style and date wearing its original costume.

- Seek advice from curators at costume and textile museums
- Draw up your own notes as to appropriate and suitable fabrics
- Always strive to replace an original costume with something fitting in style, with respect to the period of manufacture and the doll itself.

If you are dressing a baby doll then dress it as such. Nothing looks more ridiculous than what is obviously a baby doll given waist-length curls, wearing a mature frou-frou dress, and finished off with a mobcap and layers of broderie anglaise. For some obscure reason, mobcaps, and broderie anglaise trimming seem to have become popular, cheap alternatives to correct clothing. To some eyes the doll may look cute (I groan every time I see one) but this style of dress will do nothing to enhance its appeal to knowledgeable collectors or its value. Not every doll was made during the nineteenth century—a fact that seems to escape the notice of some collectors. If a doll was manufactured in the 1920s, then its hairstyle and costume should reflect that era. It is very tempting to opt for something more romantic and 'olde worlde', but try to avoid this by all means.

CATALOGUING AND DISPLAYING A COLLECTION

As many collectors have learned to their dismay, burglars now recognize the value of a doll collection. The time has gone when a thief would break into a house to steal only the silver or paintings—dolls and teddies are now prime targets and some burglars even specialize in the field. Once a bisque doll is stolen, it can be re-dressed with a different wig and outfit and look so radically different that it is very difficult to trace.

Nonetheless an up-to-date catalogue of your collection, with corresponding photographs, will
- help both you and the police if your dolls should be stolen
- provide a basis for any insurance claim for the replacement value that you may need to make
- constitute an extremely convenient and effective means of showing other collectors the type and range of dolls in your collection, without having to invite them to your home or to carry parts of your collection around the country to various meetings
- be both satisfying and great fun to do.

Mark your dolls with
- your postcode or zip code using special pens with ultraviolet-visible ink

The task of making a thorough catalogue of your collection is best accomplished as the collection is being formed. A large ring-bound folder wherein one doll is described per page is ideal, its advantage over a bound volume being that you can add to it at will—or remove pages easily if you sell or swap one of the items. Your catalogue should mention
- the type of doll and its size
- any mould numbers or distinguishing features (e.g. character doll, baby doll, boy doll)
- the probable place and date of manufacture
- eye and wig colours
- a description of the costume
- any damages or flaws to the doll
- a history of previous ownership (if known).

You should also keep a separate 'little black book', which corresponds to your main catalogue and lists when, where and from whom you bought the dolls, as well as how much they cost. In it you can keep all your receipts—and of course keep it in a safe place for security reasons.

PHOTOGRAPHING A COLLECTION
Photographs will provide you with a record of your collection year by year, and can also be a means of getting a good up-to-date valuation. You can do this by taking a selection of photographs of your better dolls to reputable auction houses for their doll experts to evaluate. Most major auctioneers provide free verbal valuations and only charge for written insurance valuations. This is a service of which many collectors are unaware and should take advantage. For the auction house it provides a welcome and useful working link with collectors, and for the collector it offers a professional and unbiased valuation. In this way you can keep abreast of current auction-room prices and thereby determine if your insurance cover is sufficient—a sensible thing to do when collecting such fragile objects.

If a doll requires re-dressing, it is also advisable to take photographs, both before and after the work has been done. When photographing your collection, bear the following points in mind
- attention paid to preparation and to careful positioning will be rewarded with better photographs
- photograph the doll indoors, and set it against a plain background
- always take the photograph from the doll's level so as to present it as an inhabitant of a world of its own scale
- each doll requires at least one individual photograph—big group shots are attractive but are not much use as a record
- the most important part of the doll is the head, so always attempt a good photograph of this
- take a full-length photograph of the dressed doll if the costume is outstanding or entirely original
- take a full-length photograph of the undressed doll if the body is unusual and of interest to collectors.

DISPLAY AND EXHIBITION
In the course of my work as a valuer for Sotheby's, I have had the pleasure of visiting many clients in their own homes, people whose collections were obviously too extensive to bring in to my office. No two collectors displayed dolls in the same way. Some like to live and work while surrounded by dolls—with dolls in the kitchen, dolls in the hall, in fact dolls almost everywhere (and often a grumpy husband unceremoniously squashed in one corner of a room with his few masculine effects). Others had jealously sealed off and securely locked one or two rooms, and only a privileged, select few were allowed to enter the secret world therein and to share and enjoy its delights. A woman I know who owns a fabulous collection never goes on holiday, hardly leaves the house, and will not even have her windows cleaned for fear of being burgled. So beware, the collecting bug can take over not only your home but your life, too, if you let it!

The way you display your dolls should reflect your tastes, character and lifestyle. For instance,
- if you have boisterous children or lively pets it is no use having your dolls on open display in a room
- locked display cabinets keep the collection out of harm's way and free from dust and cigarette smoke
- purpose-made doll stands can be purchased by mail order through doll magazines or at specialist doll fairs
- props such as miniature prams, chairs and tables help to give a more realistic and interesting environment
- how you choose to group and pose dolls—by type, size, date or personal preference—is entirely up to you.

Wherever and however you decide to display your dolls, make sure that

• they are in dry, damp-free conditions, away from sunlight

• wax or composition dolls are never displayed in cabinets with overhead internal lighting, as this will melt them

• the dolls are protected from temperature and humidity fluctuations: wax, wax-over-composition and gesso-covered dolls are particularly sensitive, and should be moved from room to room as little as possible

Dolls that are not on display can be stored away:

• wrap dolls in acid-free tissues

• always lay them face down in boxes—a doll with sleeping eyes laid on its back can result in the eyes jamming shut

• avoid plastic bags and bubble wrap—these can trap moisture over a period of time and this can cause damage to painted surfaces.

If necessity dictates that the dolls must be transported, then careful and adequate packing diminishes the risk of damage. The head is always the most fragile and most valuable part of any doll, so special care must be taken over this area. If the pate on the bisque doll is removable, carefully pack the head interior with tissue paper and then wrap the outside in suitable wadding, be it bubble wrap, cotton wadding, flanelette sheeting, or even disposable nappies (diapers). Anything that provides a thick secure barrier and can absorb shock waves in the event of a blow to the head will be fine. Transport the doll face down, pack the head interior to prevent the plaster anchorings on the eyes from loosening with vibration, and bind the body so that the limbs do not flop about. Wax dolls and dolls with porcelain arms or legs should have the limbs individually wrapped, since movement can cause them to smash together resulting in cracks and breakage. If attendance at fairs and exhibitions is a regular occurrence, be sure to incorporate adequate off-premises and in-transit insurance cover for your collection.

MAJOR MUSEUMS AND COLLECTIONS
This is not intended as a comprehensive list, but a rough guide to significant major collections in many countries. It is worth checking with the individual museums before you make your intended journey, since some museums provide limited access to their collections and others exhibit only a fraction of their inventory, and often in constantly changing exhibitions.

UNITED KINGDOM
Bethnal Green Museum, London
Birmingham Museum and Art Gallery, Birmingham
Castle Museum, York
Derbyshire County Museum, Sudbury Hall
Museum of Childhood, Edinburgh
Museum of Childhood and Costume, Blithfield Hall, near Rugeley, Staffordshire
Museum of London, London
Pollock's Toy Museum, London

Victoria and Albert Museum, London
Warwick Doll Museum, Warwick

EUROPE
Bayerisches National Museum, Munich
Dansk Folkmuseum, Copenhagen
Deutsches Spielzeugmuseum, Sonneberg
Germanisches Nationalmuseum, Nuremberg
Haags Gemeentemuseum, The Hague
Legoland Museum, Billund, Denmark
Musée des Arts Décoratifs, Paris
Musée d'Histoire de l'Education, Paris
National Museum of Finland, Helsinki
Norsk Folkmuseum, Oslo
Rijksmuseum, Amsterdam
Städtische Kunstsammlungen, Augsburg

UNITED STATES OF AMERICA
The Brooklyn Children's Museum, Brooklyn, New York
Cameron's Doll Museum, Colorado
Detroit Children's Museum, Detroit, Michigan
Essex Institute, Salem, Massachusetts
Mary Merrit's Doll Museum, Douglasville
Museum of the City of New York, New York, New York
Plymouth Antiquarian Society, Plymouth, Massachusetts
Smithsonian Institution, Washington, D.C.
Margaret Woodbury Strong Museum, Rochester, New York
Washington Dolls' House & Toy Museum, Washington, D.C.
Wisconsin State Historical Society, Madison, Wisconsin

RECOMMENDED READING
The Collector's Encyclopaedia of Dolls Dorothy S., Elizabeth A., and Evelyn J. Coleman (Robert Hale)
The Collector's History of Dolls Constance Eileen King (Robert Hale)
Dolls John Noble (Studio Vista)
Dolls and Dolls Houses Kay Desmonde (Letts)
Dolls and Doll Makers Mary Hillier (Weidenfeld and Nicolson)
Lenci Dolls Dorothy S. Coleman (Hobby House Press)
Pollocks History of English Dolls (Robert Hale)

BUYER'S GUIDE

From time to time one or two collectors emerge who possess seemingly unlimited financial resources, can buy almost anything they want, build up fine collections almost overnight, and are a joy to dealers and auction rooms alike. Such people are rare. Most people build up their collections over a long period of time after careful budgeting, planning, and making a considerable investment in time and research that results in greater confidence and experience. When building up a collection, you might make mistakes—mistakes that can later prove costly—but it is important not to dwell on these but to learn from them so that they are not repeated.

If you are about to start a collection I suggest that before you start spending you take some time to read and visit as many doll collections as possible. Many specialist books have appeared in the past decade, and more specific research has been done into manufacturers and historical details of doll production. Usually, however, lavishly illustrated books (unlike this one) tend to concentrate solely on the least obtainable and least affordable types of dolls available, but at least this compact volume will give you something to aim for. Dolls donated to museums are often of the more ordinary type and will give a better idea of relative rarity and of the great variety of dolls now collected. In addition to this you could attend the viewing days of a major doll auction, which will allow you not only to see the dolls with their wigs removed, but to have a chance to handle them without any pressure to buy. Your first forays may be to view the dolls in order to observe and compare the dolls on offer, and then to follow through by comparing the prices obtained for them. In this way you will become familiar with the types of doll offered, their relative flaws and values, and be better armed to spot anomalies or discrepancies that you may encounter when buying from dealers or private individuals. You can also find out which dolls appeal to you the most, and by keeping an eye on sale prices you can gauge whether they are within your price range or not.

If you have limited funds, it is best to decide on one type or theme of doll in which to specialize:

• dolls made from the same material, such as wax dolls by different makers
• fashion dolls wearing original costumes
• dolls of different materials but of the same date
• dolls made by a particular manufacturer, such as Kestner, Simon & Halbig, or Jumeau.

Some collectors prefer Oriental or black dolls, others exclusively collect huge child-like dolls (and presumably live in houses with castle-like proportions in order to house them).

Many collectors in the past simply acquired one doll after another, no matter what came to hand; their collections lack any central theme and are a conglomeration of assorted doll types that are often duplicated. This is fine so long as the dolls are inexpensive or were gifts, but once serious capital is invested more thought needs to be employed. It is easier to specialize these days as dolls are more readily available, whether through specialist dealers, auction rooms, or collectors' clubs. Always aim for quality rather than quantity in your collection, do not be afraid to sell duplicates, and aim to upgrade constantly. I knew two elderly sisters, both of whom had been collecting since their teens. One filled a room with Armand Marseille 390 bisque dolls (probably the most commonly found bisque doll in the world), the other had about a dozen high-quality dolls—French bisque and German character dolls. When the two collections were sold the sister with the smaller collection fared much better financially than her sibling, much to the disbelief of both!

Once you have decided on a type of doll, one that you not only like but can also afford, you have to decide how to go about buying it. One way you can do this is by buying from private individuals, a satisfactory method if you are confident you know how to price dolls and will not be either overcharged or cheating the person selling it to you. Since the public at large now has a heightened awareness of doll values (often unrealistically high expectations of value resulting from ignorance and watching too many antiques programmes on television!), local advertising for old dolls may not have the success rate it once did.

BUYING AT AUCTION

If you attend specialist doll auctions, you will need to order the catalogue, attend the viewing day, and bid at the sale. This can be exciting, nerve-racking, and, depending on whether your bid is successful or not, either extremely exhilarating or dreadfully disappointing. Buying at auction has both advantages and disadvantages.

Advantages:
- lavishly illustrated catalogues containing full descriptions and printed estimates serve as a guide to buyers
- doll experts have to be scrupulously honest and fair in their dealings
- major auction houses maintain high professional standards and integrity
- you can ask for a doll expert from the auction house to bid on your behalf if you are unable to attend the auction
- you can build up a relationship with the specialists, who will come to know your likes and dislikes and may advise you against certain dolls they think would be unsuitable
- unless competition is particularly fierce, the doll will usually be less expensive than if it were bought from a dealer (who has to add on a profit margin and take into account business costs when retailing a doll).

Disadvantages:
- viewing and sale days are usually during the week, when most people are at work
- it is necessary to keep an eye on the various sales taking place to make sure that you receive catalogues in good time
- the responsibility ultimately falls with you to make proper checks to ensure that the doll you buy is a sound one
- it can be easy to get carried away and to bid more for a doll than you can comfortably afford

- you can be left bitterly disappointed if someone bids more than you (I still bear fond memories of the ones that got away!).

Bidding in the auction room is not the mysterious, difficult process that it is often made out to be. You do not have to develop a squint, a wink, or any other eccentric behaviour in order to bid—you just have to raise and lower your hand. I actually have met collectors who have admitted that they are terrified to enter an auction room, just in case they scratch their nose at the wrong moment and end up buying one of the lots. This does not happen. Should you genuinely make an error by bidding on the wrong lot (which happens to the most experienced bidders from time to time), do not panic but immediately draw the auctioneer's attention to this fact and the unfortunate situation can easily be remedied. Do not wait until the end of the sale or a pause in proceedings, as this will be too late and the purchase will be legally binding.

BUYING FROM A DEALER

Doll dealers take all the legwork out of collecting and obviously the price you pay will reflect all the toil and expense that has gone into providing a wide selection of dolls from which you can choose. Dealers
- take away the uncertainty that you encounter when buying at auction
- build up good relationships with their established customers and will look out for specific dolls that you need to fill gaps in your collection
- often offer a money-back arrangement, whereby if you decide you do not want your doll—even some years after the original transaction—you can offer it back at the same price you paid for it.

When purchasing your doll from a dealer it is sensible to get a receipt, which should state
- the purchase price of the doll
- the name of the manufacturer
- the mould number and date
- whether the doll is free from flaws
- exactly what work has been done on restoration and replacement.

In this way, if you later find a discrepancy you have proof to back up your complaint. Most dealers are honest and helpful, especially to a collector whose buying tastes are very specific or specialized. Unlike an auction room, a dealer may hold on to a doll if you leave a deposit and then allow you to pay by a series of instalments.

POINTS TO REMEMBER

Subtle persuasion is probably the most difficult aspect of buying to deal with, be it from a dealer trying to get you to purchase a doll or a rival bidder in an auction room trying to dissuade you from a piece. Simply follow your instincts and rely on your own judgment. If you are at all unsure, always try to give yourself a little time to consider the matter—it is better to be cautious than caught out. If you do decide that a piece is for you, then go for it and question the motives of anyone trying to dissuade you.

Whether buying a doll from an auction house, private individual, or a dealer, always observe certain rules:

• check the head for hairline cracks BEFORE YOU LEAVE THE PREMISES—damage can easily occur in transit, and auction rooms will refuse to accept the return of a doll once you have signed for and collected it

• examine a bisque doll WITH THE WIG REMOVED—hairline cracks often occur around the crown of the head and are concealed by the wig. The only exceptions to this are dolls whose wigs are so perfect that removal may cause damage or whose wigs are so securely fixed that you may harm the head if you remove the wig. In the latter case you should aim to pay less for the doll as you are taking a risk.

Condition is all-important when buying a doll, and restoration and defects must be taken into account. Look out for

• any bisque doll with a strong, highly-coloured complexion, as pink colouring is often used to camouflage restoration

• expensive dolls in pristine condition—these may have been brilliantly restored and should be examined under an ultraviolet lamp (most large auction houses will have one of these)

• damage to the bisque hands of a Bru Jeune, which will lessen the value of the doll

• damage to dolls with porcelain limbs

• kiln dust on the face (freckle-like spots caused by dust or grime in the kiln adhering to the clay during firing)

• firing cracks

• poor colouring

• loss of original costume.

Costume is particularly important for French-produced dolls, as a significant part of their fame stems from the quality of their outfits. The other main consideration is rarity: you should expect to pay more for dolls with short production runs, and dolls made by desirable factories such as Jumeau or Bru. Generally, dolls that were expensive to buy at the time they were made will be expensive to collect now.

It has been interesting to watch as collecting trends and markets have altered and evolved since the early 1980s. At that time the star of any doll collection would have been an example of a fine French Bébé, with the names of Jumeau and Bru being uttered in hushed reverential tones, and German-produced dolls were regarded as second-best. Although fine French dolls are still strongly collected and highly revered, the German character dolls have knocked them from the pedestal they used to occupy. Dolls by Kämmer & Reinhardt, Simon & Halbig, J. D. Kestner, and Heubach can command huge sums. As specialist books on these producers appear and additional research is carried out, more collectors become fascinated and charmed by the quality, imagination, and variety of designs available. Perhaps the most desirable of all German character dolls is the 100 series. The 101, 114, 109, and 117 moulds, although expensive, are still relatively easy to obtain, but some of the remaining numbers are incredibly rare, with perhaps one or two examples known to exist; this explains the price of £90,200 ($141,600) for the 105 character doll sold by Sotheby's in February 1989.

I must add one note of caution. Whenever any object is seen to be making high prices, fakes soon appear on the market. If you come across a very rare doll at what seems to be a bargain price, scrutinize it carefully. Comparison is the best way of telling a fake from the genuine article, but this is not always possible. However, bad fakes *are* easy to spot, and even the better fakers have certain difficulties; beware of

• very bleached pale faces and unsuitable modern eyes

• ill-matched bisque heads, often with a bluish tinge

• painted details around the eyes and mouth—it is difficult to imitate the brush strokes produced by the factory worker with years of experience, and fake dolls often have overdone eyelashes, or brush strokes lacking spontaneity.

However, remember that there is a difference between reproduction dolls, made (and signed on the back of the head as such) by modern doll-makers attempting to copy a rare doll at an affordable price, and fakes, where the maker has attempted to deceive by impressing the original mould number on the back of the head.

Early wooden dolls also now make record-breaking prices, but as I have described in more detail in the earlier chapters, there is still scope for collectors of limited means. English fabric dolls, 1820s and 1830s Grödnertals, waxed composition, composition, English porcelain, and celluloid dolls are still affordable areas that the nascent collector might consider. Another important note to remember is that doll types fall in and out of fashion. The market for wax dolls in particular is subject to enormous fluctuations. One year they are highly prized, while the next they suddenly become less fashionable. It is therefore important to monitor sales as much as possible in order to seize your opportunity as soon as it arises.

The final word on acquiring your collection is that your primary goal should be to buy for pleasure, not for financial gain. Although doll collecting has so far proved a sound investment activity, with record prices achieved each year, if the bubble should burst it is important that you are left with something that gives you pleasure and satisfaction in its own right. People whose chief aim is to collect for the sheer love of a subject always have better collections than those who acquire purely for profit.

GLOSSARY

BEBE: *Type of doll representing infants up to the age of 7 years.*

BIEDERMEIER: *Style of furniture-making and decoration in Germany centred on period 1820–1830, characterized also by dolls made from papier-mâché shells and china shoulder-heads without painted or modelled hair.*

BISQUE: *Unglazed but coloured porcelain, the colour being applied before the porcelain is fired.*

CELLULOID (PYROXYLIN): *One of the early hard plastics used in the manufacture of dolls.*

COMPOSITION: *A varying mixture of paper, wood pulp, size, plaster of Paris, paste, glue and other materials.*

ENGAGEANT: *Elbow frill on a woman's gown.*

FASHION DOLL: *Doll originally distributed overseas to promote current fashions.*

FONTANGE: *Tall headdress in common use in seventeenth and eighteenth centuries.*

FURBELOW: *Decorative fabric flounces on gowns and petticoats.*

GUTTA-PERCHA: *Fibrous material, curiously confused with rubber, used in doll manufacturing in the second half of the nineteenth century.*

IMPASTO: *The application of colour in layers.*

INTAGLIO EYES: *Painted eyes with concave pupils and irises.*

MANTUA: *Loose gown worn by women in the seventeenth and eighteenth centuries.*

PAPIER-MACHE: *A mixture made chiefly of paper pulp and glue.*

PARIAN: *Hard, clear paste porcelain ideally suited for fine modelling and details; sometimes used to describe untinted bisque dolls.*

PARISIENNE: *Jumeau name for dolls with kid leather bodies.*

PUMPKIN HEAD: *Doll type made in England and Germany in 1860, typically with short blonde hair, coloured bonnets, wooden legs and arms.*

SHOULDER-HEAD: *Doll type with head, neck, shoulders and bosom made in one piece.*

SLIT-HEAD: *Waxed papier-mâché English doll produced to rival German Biedermeiers.*

STOMACHER: *Women's ornamental clothing, often decorated with jewels, worn under the bodice.*

SWIVEL-HEAD: *Doll with head that turns in neck socket in separately made shoulder-plate.*

INDEX

Page numbers in *italic* refer to the illustrations

Picture Acknowledgements
The Publishers wish to thank the following organizations for supplying photographs:

Courtesy of Christie's. © Christie's Colour Library: 74.
Courtesy of Michael Freeman: 28, 53 (below); 61 (left); 75; 77; 83 (right).

Courtesy of Claus Hansmann: 10; 11; 29; 33; 36; 39; 60; 65; 84.

Courtesy of Sotheby's London: 7; 8; 9; 12; 14; 15; 16; 17; 18; 19; 20; 21; 22; 23; 24; 25; 26; 27; 30; 31; 32; 34; 35; 37; 38; 40; 41; 42; 43; 44; 45; 46; 47; 48; 49; 50; 51; 52; 53; 54; 56; 57; 58; 59; 61 (right); 62; 63; 64; 66; 67; 68; 69; 70; 71; 72; 73; 76; 78; 80; 81; 82; 83 (left).
Courtesy of Victoria & Albert Museum: 13.